MW01196503

"While practitioners, educators, ation for the knowledge being generated in the field of neurocounseling, there has been a considerable call for clarification concerning its relevance in the everyday world of counseling professionals. By utilizing a thoroughly accessible, hands-on approach to the subject, Russell-Chapin, Pacheco, and DeFord have answered the call by providing a much-needed text underscoring how systematic, well-conceived applications of neuroscience can provide a transformative approach to counseling practice."

— **Kathryn Z. Douthit, PhD, LMHC**, professor of counseling and human development, University of Rochester

"Russell-Chapin and colleagues have provided the field with an immensely useful and functional resource that supports individualized treatment and improved client outcomes. This innovative text skillfully links neuroscience-informed interventions with targeted brain-based changes. Counseling students and professionals alike will particularly appreciate the concise introductions to brain regions and functions and clear directions for applying various transtheoretical counseling techniques."

— **Raissa Miller, PhD, LCP**, associate professor of counseling, Boise State University

"Russell-Chapin, Pacheco, and DeFord deliver a well-crafted manual for clinicians that has been sorely missing. This seamless integration of research-informed neurocounseling techniques and state-of-the-art neuroimaging helps clinicians connect presenting issues, neuroscience, therapeutic approaches, and interventions quickly and efficiently. Clinicians should keep this book close at hand at all times!"

— **Allen Novian, PhD, LPC-S, LMFT-S, BCN**, neurofeedback program coordinator, St. Mary's University

PRACTICAL NEUROCOUNSELING

Practical Neurocounseling demonstrates the importance of considering brain health in counseling, showing mental health professionals how to understand and assess the functioning of different parts of the brain without sophisticated software or intensive training.

Chapters map out individual brain areas and give tips and guidance that therapists can use to tailor their approaches to meet specific cognitive, emotional, and behavioral needs. The interventions provided in each chapter are gender and culturally neutral, with easy-to-follow directions for application. LORETA brain maps for each of the 19 brain sites help identify brain locations to brain function and areas of dysregulation, and corresponding step-by-step interventions can be used to regulate sites and behaviors.

More than just a collection of techniques, *Practical Neurocounseling* is a valuable guide for clinicians interested in the relationship between brain activity and behavior. It's also an ideal book for professors and students in any neurocounseling course and for clinicians working in talk therapy.

Lori Russell-Chapin, PhD, LCPC, BCN, is an award-winning educator and researcher at Bradley University. She has a part-time private practice in neurofeedback in Peoria, Illinois.

Nicole Pacheco, PsyD, LCP, BCB, is a neurofeedback and EEG specialist, educator, and consultant in her own private practice in Springfield, Illinois.

Jason DeFord, LCPC, is a neurofeedback specialist, educator, and counselor in a private practice in Peoria, Illinois.

PRACTICAL NEUROCOUNSELING

Connecting Brain Functions
to Real Therapy Interventions

*Edited by Lori Russell-Chapin,
Nicole Pacheco, and Jason DeFord*

Routledge
Taylor & Francis Group

NEW YORK AND LONDON

First published 2021
by Routledge
52 Vanderbilt Avenue, New York, NY 10017

and by Routledge
2 Park Square, Milton Park, Abingdon, Oxon OX14 4RN

Routledge is an imprint of the Taylor & Francis Group, an informa business

Library of Congress Cataloging-in-Publication Data
A catalog record for this title has been requested

ISBN: 978-0-367-41747-5 (hbk)
ISBN: 978-0-367-41743-7 (pbk)
ISBN: 978-0-367-82440-2 (ebk)

Typeset in Joanna
by Newgen Publishing UK

CONTENTS

EDITORS

Dr. Lori Russell-Chapin is a Professor of Counselor Education in the Department of Education, Counseling and Leadership at Bradley University in Peoria, Illinois. She earned her Ph.D. in Counselor Education from the University of Wyoming. She is an award-winning teacher and researcher at Bradley University. Currently Lori is co-director of the Center for Collaborative Brain Research, a partnership among Bradley University, OSF Saint Francis Medical Center, and the Illinois Neurological Center. Lori enjoys writing and has published and presented extensively in the local, regional, national, and international arenas. She is the author or co-author of nine books on practicum/internship, supervision, conflict resolution, grief and loss, neurofeedback, and neurocounseling. Lori is licensed in the state of Illinois as an LCPC (IL), and holds several certifications such as the Certification in Mental Health Clinical Counseling (CMHCC), Approved Clinical Supervisor (ACS), and Board Certified in Neurofeedback (BCN). She teaches clinical graduate counseling courses and is passionate about her part-time private practice with husband Dr. Ted Chapin. Dr. Russell-Chapin was named national Linda Seligman Counselor Educator of the Year by the American Mental Health Counseling Association (AMHCA). In 2017 she was honored with the international American Counseling Association Garry R. Walz Trailblazer

Award for her work with neurocounseling. In 2018 Lori was awarded the Teaching Excellence Award for the College of Education and Health Sciences. In 2020 Lori was awarded the ACA Fellow designation, the highest award through the American Counseling Association.

Dr. Nicole Pacheco, CEO/President of Professional Edge, is a licensed clinical psychologist and consultant. She specializes in performance optimization and leadership development. She obtained her doctorate in Clinical Psychology and master's in Counseling Psychology from the Adler School of Professional Psychology. She is board certified in general biofeedback and a Diplomate in Quantitative Electroencephalography (QEEG-D). She serves as adjunct faculty with Bradley University and regularly participates in speaking engagements, research, and writing. She has conducted numerous presentations, including national and international conferences. She lives in Springfield, Illinois, with her husband and two sons.

Jason DeFord is a neurofeedback specialist, educator, and counselor in a private practice in Peoria, Illinois. Jason is a Licensed Clinical Professional Counselor, and his style of therapy is to use a mixture of motivation and challenging exchanges to help clients manage the interactions of their thoughts, feelings, and behaviors. His clinical specialty includes individual, couple, and family counseling. He has experience working with children and adolescents and specializes in anger management, treatment of anxiety, depression, and post-traumatic stress disorder. He provides sex-offender treatment and works with trauma and abuse victims. Also, Jason helps clients with behavior management and stress management. He is trained in neurotherapy and is certified by the Amen Clinic as a Brain Health Coach. Jason received the 2020 Counseling Alumni Award for Innovative Practice from his counseling department at Bradley University.

CONTRIBUTORS

Mary Bartido has a B.S. in Psychology from Valdosta State University and is currently pursuing an M.A. in Clinical Mental Health Counseling at Bradley University in Peoria, Illinois.

Theodore J. Chapin, Ph.D., is a licensed clinical psychologist and owner of Chapin & Russell Associates and the Neurotherapy Institute of Central Illinois in Peoria, Illinois, for the past 30 years. He is board certified in neurofeedback (BCN).

Melissa Hodge, B.S., is a graduate student at Bradley University's Clinical Mental Health Counseling program in Peoria, Illinois. She is a Graduate Assistant at Bradley University's Counseling Research and Training Clinic Caregiver Program and a Problem-Solving Counseling Intern for Chestnut Health Systems Drug and Recovery Court Team.

Maya Ladasky lives in Indiana and is a graduate student in Clinical Mental Health Counseling at Bradley University.

Tamika Lampkin, B.A. in Psychology, has worked in the social services field for over 16 years, helping homeless families, senior citizens, and programming for youth. Tamika is currently in her last year of Clinical Mental Health Counseling at Bradley University in Peoria, Illinois.

Leah Maloney is a graduate student in Bradley University's Clinical Mental Health Counseling program. She has a B.S. from the University of Georgia in Psychology. After graduation, she plans to go into private practice.

Donna Miller, B.A., has been an elementary teacher for 17 years and is currently teaching 1st grade in Pekin, Illinois. She is also a graduate student at Bradley University in the Professional School Counseling program in Peoria, Illinois.

Christine Nave, B.S.N., R.N., is a psychiatric nurse for OSF Psychiatry and Psychology in Peoria, Illinois. She is a graduate student at Bradley University in the Master of Arts in Clinical Mental Health Counseling program.

Karoline Pitts, B.A., is living in Albuquerque, New Mexico, and enjoys learning how to bridge the gap between brain and behavior. She looks forward to incorporating neurocounseling principles into her clinical practice.

Brooke Poling, B.A., is a Clinical Mental Health Counseling student at Bradley University in Peoria, Illinois. She is an intern for the Counseling Center at Bradley University and also works as a Graduate Assistant for Bradley's Smith Career Center.

Anna Clancy Resniak has a B.A. and is a Clinical Mental Health Counseling student at Bradley University in Peoria, Illinois. Her plans after graduation are to work with adolescents and adults, specializing in trauma work.

Parneet Sahota lives in Illinois and is a graduate student in Clinical Mental Health Counseling at Bradley University.

FOREWORD

Innovative leaders of the counseling field, Russell-Chapin, Pacheco, and DeFord bring to us the most comprehensive and useful introduction to neuroscience/neurocounseling that I have seen. Having written extensively on the topic of neuroscience, I am well aware of the power of neurocounseling for applied research and clinical practice. Soon, our therapist educators will all be including ideas from this innovative and exciting book in their teaching, research, and clinical practice. I've been fascinated by each section of *Practical Neurocounseling: Connecting Brain Functions to Real Therapy Interventions.*

This co-edited book is written in clear, understandable prose, and you will gain a basic mastery of major functions of the brain. Further, this book will enable you to use these concepts in your daily practice, teaching, and research.

Here are some of the key dimensions of the book that lead the counseling/therapy field to a major paradigm shift in what these leaders have named neurocounseling:

• The Head Map of Brain Functions will give you an overview of locations and meaning of major brain areas.

- Chapter 2 turns immediately to a case study illustrating how neurocounseling will aid in seeing how various brain parts can be integrated into effective treatment planning.
- Guidelines for brain assessments are presented, which will enable you to add science findings for interviewing, planning, and treatment.
- The Head Map is reviewed in precise detail and you will learn how various client issues are associated with different brain areas and brainwave dysregulation.
- Each brain location has neurocounseling techniques to assist in regulating brainwaves in talk therapy.
- Cultural diversity issues are discussed surrounding neurocounseling.
- LORETA brain images for each of the 19 brain sites show activation in the brain as neurocounseling techniques are taught.

In short, this is a quality resource that belongs in every counselor's and therapist's office. As you observe client thinking, feeling, and behavior, it will enrich your professional work and guide you to appropriate treatment alternatives.

This book is essential as we move to a new practice in the changing future. The coronavirus (COVID-19) impacts the brain, and the accompanying stress for everyone also changes the way their brain functions. All mental issues are grounded in the brain's reaction to the surrounding environment. This book can make you a leader and add value to your counseling practice. No longer can we ignore the physiology which underlies the counseling and therapy world.

I believe this is the professional book of the year. In the future, clinical work will not be the same, and this text will be a source underlying that change. Applied science makes the difference.

I could not recommend this outstanding book more highly. Enjoy and learn!

Allen E. Ivey, EdD, ABPP
Board Certified in Counseling Psychology
Distinguished University Professor (Emeritus)
University of Massachusetts, Amherst

ACKNOWLEDGMENTS

This book is dedicated to every person, client, helping professional, researcher, student, and lay person who thinks our brain is the most incredible and fascinating master three-pound organ! Every day we learn new information about the brain and its functions. Every day it seems we dispel a few more myths about the brain. Every day we learn more about the importance of brain health. So thank you to those men and women who have donated their brains to science. That is how we learn even more. Also a very special thank you to our neuroscience and neurocounseling mentors who have encouraged us to continue on this path: Dr. Ted Chapin, Dr. Allen Ivey, John Anderson, and Douglas Dailey.

A special thank you to the editorial staff at Routledge and especially Anna Moore, our main editor, for her skills, dedication, and faith in allowing us to write this applied science brain book. Our brains need and love to be challenged. May every reader find one new piece of valuable information to keep you thriving and growing!

PART I

NEUROCOUNSELING THEORY AND KNOWLEDGE

1

UNDERSTANDING THE WORLD OF NEUROCOUNSELING AND CHAPTER SUMMARIES

Lori Russell-Chapin and Nicole Pacheco

The world of counseling has a long history of working holistically with all aspects of the human condition. For years counseling focused on the many components of wellness. *20/20: A Vision for the Future of Counseling* was first developed in 2010. After many discussions, this consensus definition stated, "Counseling is a professional relationship that empowers diverse individuals, families and groups to accomplish mental health, wellness, education and career goals" (p. 366). That is an excellent statement endorsed by 29 counseling associations (Kaplan, Tarvydas & Gladding, 2014). The counseling profession needed to go even farther.

Because of advances in neuroscience and brain imaging, we know so much more about the brain, its functions, and how the brain interacts with all components of the human system (Ivey, Ivey & Zalaquett, 2017).

Neurocounseling enters the picture with all that it has to offer. Neurocounseling does not replace counseling, but rather adds value and granular dimensions to the counseling field.

Neurocounseling was first coined by Montes (2013) from interviews with counselors around the country. Russell-Chapin (2016, p. 93) further elaborated by defining neurocounseling as "the integration of neuroscience into the practice of counseling by teaching and illustrating the physiological underpinnings of many of our mental health concerns."

I now teach basic neurocounseling skills to every client, whether that be diaphragmatic breathing, peripheral skin temperature control, heart rate variability, therapeutic lifestyle changes, and/or neuroanatomy. Recently I was working with a veteran who had been diagnosed with post-traumatic stress disorder (PTSD). Our eventual goal was to conduct neurofeedback with Tom (pseudonym), but first we worked on diaphragmatic breathing. One day he came in and started the session by saying that he and his wife got into one of their frequent fights. His typical reaction was to freeze and go into the basement. Instead, this time he just began to breathe diaphragmatically, and he calmed right down. The best part of this new response was "My wife almost fainted because I didn't run away. I was amazed too. We actually talked about our problem." I am constantly reminded of one of my favorite Chinese sayings, "Give a man a fish, and he will eat for a day. Teach a man to fish, and he will eat for a lifetime." That is the power of neurocounseling.

Therefore, instead of emphasizing mental illness and mental health, it makes more sense to emphasize brain illness and brain health. Neurocounseling affords counselors the opportunity to do so by examining more deeply the neuroanatomy of our bodies and its impact on overall physical and emotional health. For example, when people go to their internists, often all the various bodily functions are checked. When patients go to the pulmonologist, the lungs are looked at and examined. When patients go to the cardiologist, the heart is often tested and observed. When clients go to a psychiatrist, psychologist, counselor, and social worker, we don't look at the brain. We do listen to our clients' thoughts and emotions, which is essential to counseling. We also need to be looking at the brain and body. Counselors now have the capabilities to do just that … examine and look at the brain and its brainwaves! Understanding how each of our client's brains functions affords the mental health professional the opportunity to create truly individualized treatment plans. Neurocounseling assists us to be more efficacious and successful with additional measurable outcomes and goals.

This neurocounseling technique book, *Practical Neurocounseling: Connecting Brain Functions to Therapy Interventions*, offers applied techniques to those who want and need to integrate brain-based approaches into their clinical counseling practices. Treatment success can be reached much more quickly and efficiently by a neurocounseling-informed therapist who not only understands how a client experiences his or her world, but can connect this information to more fully understand how the client's brain is functioning (Field, Jones & Russell-Chapin, 2017). Thereby, the therapist is able to create and implement a treatment plan and follow a successful course of therapy that is attainable and suitable to each individual patient. For example, a patient diagnosed with an autism spectrum disorder (ASD) has a brain that communicates and functions differently than that of a patient who is not diagnosed with a disorder on the autism spectrum. This client's brain suffers from dysregulation in the anterior cingulate and orbitofrontal regions that leads to problems in the areas of emotional regulation, attention, and executive functions. In addition, he or she will struggle to correctly identify and understand the emotions and intentions of others, creating a vicious cycle (Thompson & Thompson, 2015). Also, the brain of a war veteran suffering from PTSD is likely to show hyperactivation or overarousal in the areas of the brain tied to hypervigilance and hypoactivation, or under-arousal, in mediation areas of the brain. As a result, unlike a regulated brain that is able to correctly interpret events, people, and things in their environment, the brain of the war veteran may be constantly on edge and incorrectly interpreting environmental cues as dangerous or threatening when they are not (Thompson & Thompson, 2015).

The purpose and goal of this book is to provide effective, neurologically sound interventions for mental health professionals. With as much interest and detail as we explore the internal processes (e.g., thoughts, feelings, behaviors), professionals can add an additional layer of understanding by conceptualizing areas of concern to their neurological derivations. Likewise, brain assessment surveys are also of critical value in understanding the world of the client and just as relevant as asking about family of origin issues and substance use. Brain assessment surveys and tools will be discussed later in Chapter 3.

Therapists can understand and assess the functioning of different parts of a client's brain without sophisticated software or intensive training.

Often, the addition of a simple paper-and-pencil brain-based symptom checklist is a quick and easy addition to the intake assessment. Once the therapist has this understanding, treatment can be tailored to meet the client's cognitive, emotional, and behavioral level. It also serves as a blueprint to support the areas of the brain that are doing well and to stimulate and encourage growth in the areas that are underfunctioning. The interventions in this book are gender and culturally neutral, with easy-to-follow directions for applications. This text will be a valuable resource for professors, students, and clinicians.

The co-editors of this book just completed teaching our graduate-level ENC 607 Bridging Brain and Behavior course to 22 online students and 14 campus-based students. The online students attended their residency at Bradley University in Peoria, Illinois. We combined poster presentations from all the students and held an informative exhibition of techniques for all 19 Head Map of Functions and locations of the brain. It was an incredible experience, thus the origins and birth of this textbook.

An example of the Head Map of Function (Anderson, 2020) is included below, so the reader can get a better visual of all these neurocounseling sites, functions, and techniques, which can be integrated into our counseling world (Figure 1.1). This graphic will be at the beginning of each chapter and function, depicting the exact site with a bolded circle. The remainder of Chapter 1 will summarize the chapters for the rest of the book.

Chapter 2: The Case of Patrice: Struggling for Stability and Independence

This chapter will focus on a case study to demonstrate how neurocounseling and neuroanatomy can be integrated in all aspects of a client's life. Cognitions, behaviors, emotions, interpersonal relationships, environmental factors – these are just a few of the factors and areas that mental health providers regularly assess and evaluate when dealing with clients. Making changes in one or more of these areas with the assistance of a supportive provider often leads to success. But how long do these improvements last? How often do you see clients getting themselves out of one hole to fall into another?

Mental health professionals are highly trained and skilled in attentively listening and responding to clients in a nonjudgmental, helpful

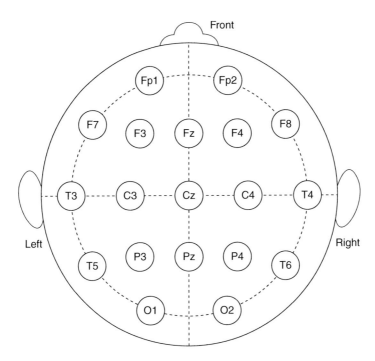

Figure 1.1 Head Map of Functions

manner. However, this training is often based in psychological theory of thoughts, feelings, and behaviors while influencing and interacting with one another. Mental health professionals become fluent in identifying unwanted thoughts, emotions, and behaviors and guiding the client to replace them with more helpful or effective thoughts, feelings, and behaviors. We instruct our clients on how to replicate this outside the session. However, a pitfall of using this approach alone is that changing the underlying source of these internal processes often goes ignored.

The brain's anatomy and physiology are quite impressive, but this knowledge provides little help to providers when they are sitting in front of a severely depressed client who doesn't care about their brain's anatomy but is desperately seeking refuge from internal pain. However, short- and long-term success can be achieved more quickly and successfully when there is a synthesis between the neurophysiological underpinnings of what is occurring in this client's brain and effective, neurophysiological-based clinical interventions that address the root of the problems, the brain.

Chapter 3: Assessment, Treatment Planning, and Outcome Evaluation

In this chapter the reader will learn that assessing brain function can be done in a variety of ways. Valuable information can be obtained from self-report questionnaires, computerized tests, and, of course, advanced methods by actually looking at brain-wave activity, electroencephalography (EEG), and comparing this information to databases, such as Paul Swingle's Clinical Q or a 19-channel EEG (Collura & Frederick, 2017) that assesses each of the International Classification's 10–20 sites. Table 1.1 describes the pros and cons of different assessment tools and the areas that they each assess.

Chapter 4: Prefrontal Cortex (FP1 and FP2): Leading with the CEO of the Brain

This chapter will focus on the prefrontal cortex (sites FP1 and FP2), home to the executive functions, which allows us to control our attention, decrease or eliminate unwanted behavior, and engage in planning, organization, and effective decision making. Dysregulation factors and two neurocounseling techniques will be presented for each site. LORETA (Collura & Frederick, 2017) image activations will be shown for each site.

Left Prefrontal Cortex (FP1)

FP1 Location: The FP1 location of the brain is on the left side of the frontal lobe, located in the far front, covered by the prefrontal cortex. The frontal lobe is the largest of the four brain lobes. It is part of the cerebral cortex, has paired lobes (the left and right), which comprise two-thirds of the human brain.

FP1 Function(s): FP1 plays an important role in attention, concentration, decision making, emotions, mood, planning, task completion, visual episodic retrieval, and visual working memory (Carter, 2014; Chapin & Russell-Chapin, 2014). The prefrontal cortex involves a higher level of cognition; it is part of the cerebral cortex, which covers the front portion of the frontal lobe. The prime activity of this region is considered to be a choreography of thoughts and actions in collaboration with internal

Table 1.1 Pros and cons of different assessment tools

Test	Areas or Functions Assessed	Pros	Cons
Dr. Daniel Amen's Free Brain Health Assessment	Comprehensive Overview of Brain.	• Free • Available online or paper and pencil	• Bias due to nature of self-report questionnaire (however, significant others can also rate the patient)
Neurological Dysregulation Risk Assessment (Chapin & Russell-Chapin)		• Quick and easily to complete	-
TOVA (Test of Variable Attention)	Types of Attention	• Frequently used in research	• Long and difficult for those with severe attention problems
Clinical Q (Paul Swingle)		• Compares client to a clinical database	
19-Channel EEG	• Comprehensive assessment of cortical electrical activity • Generates z-scores (compared to others of same age and sex)	• Comprehensive	• Time (1 hour for recording and additional time to review, analyze, and interpret information) • Cost

goals. In addition, this area is known as the executive function of the brain as it can differentiate among conflicting thoughts, such as good vs. bad or different vs. same.

Dysregulation: Factors attributed to brain dysregulation in FP1 may include: genetics, diet and exercise, stress, trauma/injuries, abusive relationships, toxins, and substance abuse (Chapin & Russell-Chapin, 2014). Common mental health diagnoses associated with dysregulation in the frontal lobe/prefrontal cortex are the following: depression, attention deficit hyperactivity disorder (ADHD), obsessive-compulsive disorder (OCD), schizophrenia, bipolar disorder, traumatic brain injury, personality disorders, and post-traumatic stress disorder (PTSD). Damage to the frontal lobe can cause the following symptoms: speech problems, poor coordination, changes in personality, and difficulties with impulse control, planning, or sticking to a schedule (Villines, 2017). Individuals with frontal lobe damage may struggle with processing information, remembering previous experiences, and making decisions.

Right Prefrontal Cortex (FP2)

FP2 Location: The frontal lobe is the largest of the four lobes that make up the human brain. The prefrontal cortex is located in the front part of the frontal lobe. It is a ribbon of thick grey matter that can be divided into three regions: the dorsolateral, orbital, and ventromedial regions. The prefrontal cortex is comprised of different kinds of neurons that are communicated to various regions of the brain (Tamminga, 2004) and is connected to the thalamus, the basal ganglia, and the brainstem (Fuster, 2004).

FP2 Function(s): High-order actions occur in the prefrontal cortex of the brain (Carter, 2014). High-order actions, referred to as executive function, may include personality expression, planning and executing behavior, and decision making (Dahlitz, 2017). Further, executive function is connected to the human's ability to discern conflicting thoughts, decide what is good and bad, determine consequences, work toward an identified goal, and operate within social norms (Dahlitz, 2017). Individuals who suffer from mental health issues, those who abuse cannabis, and repeated stressors can reduce communication between the frontal lobe and other regions of the brain. A well-functioning prefrontal cortex may be responsible for feelings of guilt and be able to reduce anxiety (Dahlitz, 2017).

Dysregulation: Dysregulation in the prefrontal cortex, specifically the FP2, can present as emotional issues, irritability, impulsivity, or panic behavior.

Chapter 5: Frontal Lobes: Seeing the Trees and Seeing the Forest for the Trees

This chapter will focus on the frontal lobes, which are involved in a number of highly sophisticated and important functions. In general, the left frontal lobe is connected to communication skills (verbal and written) and understanding the sequence of events. The healthy functioning of the left frontal lobe allows us to focus on details and data. Likewise, generally speaking, the right frontal lobe helps us "see the whole picture" and synthesize the smaller pieces of information in an appropriate and useful manner. Dysregulation, LORETA images, and two neurocounseling techniques will be offered.

F3

F3 Location: The motor cortex is located at the posterior region of the frontal lobe, extending along the anterior of the Rolandic fissure. The Sylvian fissure separates the motor cortex from the temporal lobes.

F3 Function(s): F3 is responsible for motor planning, right upper extremities, fine motor coordination for the right side of the body, visual episodic retrieval, mood elevation, object processing, emotional interpretation, and positive mood (Russell-Chapin 2016). The motor cortex is responsible for receiving information from the other lobes in the brain. This information is then utilized to carry out bodily movements (Bergland, n.d.).

Dysregulation: Dysregulation of F3 may appear as problems with gross and fine motor planning of right lower extremities, retrieval of visual information, emotion (depression, negative thoughts), and interpreting the emotions of others.

Right Frontal Lobe (F4)

F4 Location: Brain site F4 is located in the posterior section of the frontal lobe in the right hemisphere.

F4 Function: It is the site called the motor cortex, which is responsible for premotor and motor functions, such as motor planning, coordination, and movement execution of the left extremities (Chapin & Russell-Chapin, 2014). Motor planning is the coordination and mental rehearsal of movement (Sheahan, Franklin & Wolpert, 2016). F4 is also active in fine motor coordination of the left extremities (Chapin & Russell-Chapin, 2014), which is how certain muscle groups work together to complete specific tasks, such as the muscles active in touching your thumb to your index finger or wiggling your toes.

This site in the brain is also active in semantic and episodic verbal retrieval, or the translation of thoughts, knowledge, and memories into spoken words (Chapin & Russell-Chapin, 2014; Swingle, 2016). Attention, impulse, and emotional regulation are also functions of brain site F4 (Swingle, 2016).

Dysregulation: Individuals experiencing trouble regulating attention, impulses, and emotions are indicators of dysregulation at the F4 location. F4 is activated in cognitive and emotional tasks, such as planning, task completion, organizing, and sequencing, as well as emotional stability or volatility. Time-management, or the ability to organize tasks and the completion of such tasks in a manner that utilizes time efficiently, is an activity associated with brain site F4. Effective regulation of attention and impulse are crucial for successful time management because it requires focus on the task at hand without distraction, as well as organizing the self in such a manner that the necessary resources to complete the task are available or accessible to the individual.

Dysregulation at brain site F4 may present in physical symptoms related to motor planning and control. This may manifest as messy or illegible handwriting, particularly if left-hand dominant. Dysregulation at F4 may also manifest in motor coordination issues related to dexterity, such as hand gripping or readiness to perform specific physical tasks like catching a ball or unlocking a door with a key. Physical dyspraxia is often found in children with developmental delays and individuals on the autism spectrum, and is manifested in delays in motor planning and execution (Gibbs, Appleton & Appleton, 2007).

Dysregulation at brain site F4 may be manifested as verbal apraxia, or disorganized speech. This condition is common in children with developmental delays, as well as individuals with ADHD and individuals on the autism spectrum (Printz, Mehlum & Nikoghosyan-Bossen, 2018; Schumacher, Strand & Augustyn, 2017). Verbal apraxia is a difficulty in the motor planning necessary to produce speech, such as the syllables, tones, and sounds that create recognized language.

Midline Frontal Lobe (FZ)

FZ Location: FZ is located between the nasion/nase and CZ, the midsection of the skull.

FZ Function: FZ assists with motor planning of both lower extremities. It helps with emotional inhibition and grooming. Often with dysregulation at FZ, there is too much high beta, so fretting and obsessional compulsive symptoms may occur.

Dysregulation: Dysregulation problems at FZ may show as attentional and motivational concerns.

Left Frontal Lobe (F7)

F7 Location: F7 is located in the left hemisphere of the brain directly to the left of FZ. This is where the Broca Area is found.

F7 Function(s): The main function of F7 is verbal expression and speech fluency. Mood regulation may be a part of F7, along with visual and auditory working memory. Too many theta waves in F7 will often find clients with difficulty in locating certain words.

Dysregulation: Dysregulation at F7 may show problems with input control and some speech concerns.

Right Frontal Lobe (F8)

F8 Location: The F8 location is in the right hemisphere of the frontal lobe directly to the right of FZ.

F8 Function: The function of this area is as follows: the motor cortex is responsible for making movements, while the premotor cortex selects the movements. The prefrontal cortex controls cognitive processes. This will allow the correct movements to be made at the correct time and place, and these specific selections of movements are made through external or internal cues, self-knowledge, or in response of something. F8 also assists in emotional expression, drawing, endogenous mood regulation, face recognition, emotional processing, visual/spatial working memory, and sustained attention.

Dysregulation: Dysregulation at F8 may involve prosody and oversensitivity to others' speech intonation.

Chapter 6: Sensory Motor (C3, CZ, and C4): Making the World Move

This chapter features the sensory motor strip. Functions, dysregulation, LORETA images, and two neurocounseling interventions will be showcased.

CZ Location: CZ is located in the center of the head at the midline. It is situated in the sensory and motor cortices, which are divided by a large groove called the central sulcus. The motor cortex is located at the back of the frontal lobe, and controls motor movements by sending direct and indirect signals to the muscles. The sensory cortex is located in the parietal lobe, and it takes in sensory input from the environment. The parietal lobe is utilized mainly for body orientation and awareness of body position, spatial awareness, and attention. Both the frontal and parietal lobes may be utilized when executing a movement, depending on whether or not the movement is conscious or unconscious.

CZ is situated directly above the basal ganglia, which are a bundle of nuclei in the base of the forebrain that act as a filter for selecting and mediating movements, as well as implementing movement routines. The basal ganglia contain structures including the globus pallidus, putamen, striatum, and substantia nigra. These structures are integral in motor control and muscle movement. CZ is a brain area that is related to sensation and movement, both in terms of location and in terms of function.

CZ Function: There are various different functions that are related to CZ, many of which are related to sensations and movement. CZ is located in the sensory and motor cortices, and therefore many of its functions are related to the integration of sensory input and motor output. Because CZ spans both the frontal and parietal lobes, it is important for conscious thought and planning for motor movement, as well as sensory information and body position awareness. CZ also acts as a thalamic efferent by taking information from the thalamus, a brain area that filters and relays sensory information to various parts of the brain. CZ is important for a person's sensorimotor rhythm and ability to coordinate sensory input with motor output and movements. It also functions to allow people to have awareness of their body position and movements.

Dysregulation: Dysregulation at CZ may cause hyperactivity and motivational problems.

Left Central (C3)

C3 Location: The C3 location is in the central lobe between CZ and T3. C3 communicates with many different parts of the brain that leads it to being responsible for many different functions.

C3 Function: Its biggest responsibility is for the sensorimotor integration of the right upper extremities, i.e., the right arm, hand, etc., but is also tied to handwriting, short-term memory, and the alerting responses.

Dysregulation: When dysregulation of the C3 occurs, there is impaired sensorimotor integration in the client. Proper sensorimotor integration allows the client to respond appropriately with predicted sensory feedback and motor commands. High levels of theta in the C3 would be displayed in poor handwriting, whereas high levels of beta in the C3 would show as motor hyperactivity.

Right Central (C4)

C4 Location: C4 is located in the central brain in the right hemisphere found behind the sulcus in the sensory area.

C4 Function: The main functions of the C4 location in the brain are sensorimotor integration, assistance in calming, left-handedness, and short-term memory production. The main cause of dysregulation in C4 is increased levels of beta waves. When a human brain experiences increased levels of beta in C4, the main manifestation is seen as hypervigilance (Chapin & Russell-Chapin, 2014). Of all the functions of C4, sensorimotor integration is affected the most by increased levels of beta.

Dysregulation: When sensorimotor integration is dysregulated, sensory input is not integrated or organized in the proper ways, and can lead to the diagnosis of autism.

Chapter 7: Temporal Lobes (T3, T4, T5, and T6): The Integration of the World, Myself, and Others

This chapter emphasizes the temporal lobes. Functions, dysregulations, and two neurocouneling techniques for each site will be shown. The left and right temporal lobes are critical in understanding and interpreting tonality, sounds, and other auditory information. In addition, temporal lobes function as important integration centers that allow us to incorporate new information with old information.

Left Temporal (T3)

T3 Location: T3 is located in the left anterior temporal lobe, behind the ear.

T3 Function: Regionally, the temporal lobe is typically associated with such processes as language comprehension, sensory input, and memory retention. T3, specifically, has several associated functions, including verbal memory formation and storage, phonological processes, hearing, and the ability to remember what you see.

Dysregulation: People experiencing high concentrations of beta waves in T3 will present with several symptoms or areas of concern, including memory problems, lack of flexible memory, and trouble processing language. People experiencing high concentrations of theta waves may present with concerns such as irritability, stress, and apathy.

Right Temporal (T4)

T4 Location: The brain site for T4 is in the right hemisphere of the cerebral cortex. It is specifically located in the primary auditory cortex of the forward section of the right temporal lobe by the right ear.

T4 Function: First, the temporal lobe is responsible for objective recognition, emotion, and memory. Next, the right hemisphere of the cerebral cortex is responsible for sensory input, creative abilities, awareness of visual and auditory input, and the spatial-temporal awareness of what is happening in the environment second by second. The primary auditory cortex located in the temporal lobe is responsible for processing the sounds picked up by the ears. More specifically, in the primary auditory cortex of the right temporal lobe, is the region T4. The main function of region T4 is forming and storing emotional and autobiographical memory. It contributes to the development of personality, as well as the ability to hear, recognize patterns, organize, and create music. T4 notices and interprets the melody, and the tone and affective quality of voice. It contributes to the ability to vary singing and tone, as well as recall melodies and emotionally charged experiences. It helps one to notice when something speaks to or resonates with the listener. It also helps one to sense when another is speaking in a false or phony way. In other words, T4 weighs the intent implied in the tone of the voice. When the bad intent is heard, T4 helps manage hostile reactions. Thus, T4 has been suggested to be the Emotive Listener.

Dysregulation: Too much theta at T4 may be displayed as sadness and/ or anger.

Left Temporal (T5)

T5 Location: T5 is located in the left temporal lobe of the brain.

T5 Function: The temporal lobes assist with working memory, comprehension of word meaning (Wernicke area), integration of new information, retrieval of words, and the emotional valence of thoughts and behavior including temper control. It also assists with short-term memory, inner voice, and logical and verbal understanding.

Dysregulation: Dysregulation in the left temporal lobe can involve aggression, violent thoughts, sensitivity to provocation, paranoia, decreased verbal memory, and emotional instability. More specifically, increased theta waves can cause decreased understanding of meaning, spontaneity, and inattention, and elevated beta waves lead to increased confusion, effortful reading, and problems finding meaning.

Right Temporal (T6)

T6 Location: T6 is in the temporal lobe and located to the right of P4.

T6 Function: The main function of T6 is better emotional understanding through facial and symbol recognition. Long-term memory is activated here, and excessive theta waves interfere with this function.

Dysregulation: Dysregulation at T6 may be displayed in poor memory of faces and even musical melodies.

Chapter 8: Parietal Lobes (P3, PZ, and P4) – Making Sense of One's Experience and the World Around Me

The parietal lobes play an important role in the areas of visual acuity and pattern recognition. They also help us make sense of raw sensory material and turn this information into useful perceptions.

Central Parietal (PZ)

PZ Location: PZ is located in the parietal lobe directly behind CZ.

PZ Function: PZ has the main function of spatial relations and attentional shifting.

Dysregulation: Too much high beta will often cause persevering thoughts and hypervigilance.

Left Parietal (P3)

P3 Location: P3 is located on the left side of the head directly to the left of PZ and in between T5 and PZ.

P3 Function: The main function of P3 is to regulate the right side of perception and spatial relations.

Dysregulation: Dysregulation may be displayed as problems with memory, recalling numbers, and disorganized thinking.

Right Parietal (P4)

P4 Location: P4 is located in the right the temporal lobe directly to the right of PZ.

P4 Function: The main function of P4 is to work with the left side of the head with spatial relations and cognitive processing.

Dysregulation: Sometimes an overactivated P4 will cause a client to have a victim mentality, so again working on emotional and physiological safety is important here. Too much theta will often allow a client to focus too much on self and ruminate.

Chapter 9: Occipital Lobes (O1 and O2): Visualizing the World through Recognition and Patterns

The left and right occipital lobes play a crucial role in our interpretation and recognition of visual information, as well as being home to one of the most important "resting rhythms" of the brainwave (commonly referred to as posterior dominant rhythm).

Left Occipital (O1)

O1 Location: The occipital lobes are the rearmost lobes of the forebrain. The internal view of the occipital lobe in the human brain is not marked by any clear confines and it usually pinpointed by the occipital bone of the skull. O1 is in the left hemisphere.

O1 Function: The occipital lobes consist of various visual areas, which contain a map of the ocular world. O1 is responsible for the processing of information associated with the right side of vision, pattern recognition, color, movement, black and white and edge perception, visual acuities, operational and measurable memories, and dreams. The visual consciousness of depth and edge, as well as perception about things, places, and people, is essential in day-to-day navigation, safety, and security of the person and their dependents. O1 also holds the responsibility for reading, writing, spelling, comprehension of both reading and writing, drawing, identification of objects, and recognition of places and their associations to self.

Dysregulation: Dysregulation in the occipital lobes may cause difficulties with pattern recognition.

Right Occipital (O2)

O2 Location: The occipital lobes are the rearmost lobe of the forebrain. The internal view of the occipital lobe in the human brain is not marked by any clear confines and it usually pinpointed by the occipital bone of the skull. O2 is in the right hemisphere.

O2 Function: O2 is responsible for the processing of information associated with the left side of vision, pattern recognition, color, movement, black and white and edge perception, visual acuities, operational and measurable memories, and dreams. The visual consciousness of depth and edge, as well as perception about things, places, and people, is essential in day-to-day navigation, safety, and security of the person and their dependents. O2 also holds the responsibility for reading, writing, spelling, comprehension of both reading and writing, drawing, identification of objects, and recognition of places and their associations to self.

Chapter 10: Conclusions: Coming Full Circle

This summary chapter discusses how all of these neurocounseling interventions may be used in regular talk therapy sessions. It will consolidate the interconnectivity of the brain, and show the importance of understanding the brain and its functions to overall counseling effectiveness.

Conclusions

This first chapter introduces and defines neurocounseling and discusses the added value to the counseling profession and its impact on our clients. A summary of the book chapters is delivered to help the reader envision the entire text and its uses.

References

Anderson, J.A. (2020). Personal Communication, Head Map of Functions. Quantitative EEG (qEEG). (2014). Retrieved from www.aboutneurofeedback. com/neurofeedback-info-center/information-for-clinicians/adding-neurofeedback-to-a-practice/quantitative-eeg-qeeg/.

Bergland, C. (n.d.). Alpha brain waves boost creativity and reduce depression. Retrieved March 17, 2018 from www.psychologytoday.com/blog/the-athletes-way/201504/alpha-brain-waves-boost-creativity-and-reduce-depression.

Carter, R. (2014). *The Human Brain Book* (rev. ed.). New York: DK Publishing.

Chapin, T.J. & Russell-Chapin, L.A. (2014). *Neurotherapy and Neurofeedback: Brain-based treatment for psychological and behavioral problems*. New York: Routledge.

Collura, T.F. & Frederick, J.A. (eds.). (2017). *Handbook of Clinical QEEG and Neurotherapy*. New York: Routledge.

Dahlitz, M. (2017). Prefrontal cortex. *Neuroscience*. Retrieved from www.thescienceofpsychotherapy.com/prefrontal-cortex/.

Field, T., Jones, L. & Russell-Chapin, L. (2017). *Neurocounseling: Brain-based clinical approaches*. Alexandria, VA: American Counseling Association.

Fuster, J.M. (2001). The prefrontal cortex – An update. *Neuron* 30(2), 319–333.

Gibbs, J., Appleton, J. & Appleton, R. (2007). Dyspraxia or developmental coordination disorder? Unravelling the enigma. *Archives of Disease in Childhood* 92(6), 534–539.

Ivey, A., Ivey, M.B. & Zalaquett, C. (2017). *Intentional Interviewing and Counseling in a Multicultural Society.* (9th ed). Boston, MA: Cengage Learning.

Kaplan, D.M., Tarvydas, V.M. & Gladding, S. (2014). 20/20: A vision of the future of counseling: The new consensus definition of counseling. *Journal of Counseling and Development* 7(92), 366–372. DOI:10.1002/j.1556- 6676.2014.00164.x.

Montes, S. (2013, December). The birth of the neurocounselor. *Counseling Today* 56(6), 32–40.

Printz, T., Mehlum, C.S. & Nikoghosyan-Bossen, G. (2018). Verbal and oral dyspraxia in children and juveniles. *Ugeskrift for laeger* 180(12).

Russell-Chapin, L.A. (2016). Integrating neurocounseling into the counseling profession: An introduction. *Journal of Mental Health Counseling* 38(2), 93–102. DOI:10.17744/mehc.38.2.01.

Schumacher, J., Strand, K.E. & Augustyn, M. (2017). Apraxia, autism, attention-deficit hyperactivity disorder: do we have a new spectrum? *Journal of Developmental & Behavioral Pediatrics* 38, S35–S37.

Sheahan, H.R., Franklin, D.W. & Wolpert, D.M. (2016). Motor planning, not execution, separates motor memories. *Neuron* 92(4), 773–779.

Swingle, P.G. (2016). *Adding Neurotherapy to Your Practice: Clinician's guide to the ClinicalQ, neurofeedback, and braindriving.* New York: Springer.

Tamminga, C.A. (2004). Structure of the human prefrontal cortex. *American Journal of Psychiatry* 161(8). https://doi.org/10.1176/appi.ajp.161.8.1366.

Thompson, M. & Thompson, L. (2015). *The Neurofeedback Book* (2nd Ed.). Wheat Ridge, CO: Association for Applied Psychophysiology and Biofeedback (www.aapb.org).

Villines, Z. (2017). Frontal lobe: Functions, structure, and damage. Retrieved from www.medicalnewstoday.com/articles/318139.php.

2

DEMONSTRATING NEUROCOUNSELING AND NEUROANATOMY WITH THE CASE OF PATRICE

Struggling with Stability and Independence

Lori Russell-Chapin

The Case of Patrice: Struggling for Stability and Independence

The purpose of this case study is to help the reader integrate neurocounseling and neurofeedback practices into regular talk therapy. Basic neuroanatomy will also be discussed, for which all clients could benefit.

This chapter will introduce the reader to a young woman who was very dysregulated and struggling to survive. The first day Patrice and I met each other, she noticed a small saying on my wall, "It takes courage to grow up and become who you really are," written by the poet, ee cummings. Patrice inquired about its meaning. I asked her what she thought it meant. We began discussing briefly about how much courage it takes to come into counseling to make life changes and that sometimes we might even have to get rid of or adapt some of our personal beliefs given to us by others. Patrice seemed intrigued.

That was our beginning. I learned that Patrice is a 23-year-old Caucasian female who is college educated and was referred to our clinic by a family member. She reluctantly came to the session from a 30-day residential treatment center for bipolar episodes of mania, delusions, and bizarre behaviors.

Patrice (Pat) was dressed casually yet hygienically appropriate. She is now living with her immediate family. Her mother attended the first meeting, and it was painfully clear there was tension between the two of them. They both recounted the history of struggles for Pat. There have been historical episodes of mania and grandiosity. This time seemed escalated with rambling speech and loss of reality. I then asked Mom to step out of the room, so I could get to know Pat better. I asked Pat to give me a Release of Information from the hospital, and she refused. Once Pat realized I was on her side as an ally, she signed the Release of Information. The records were obtained and were thorough. The attending psychiatrist at the hospital had diagnosed Patrice with Bi-Polar 1 Disorder, Current with Psychotic features, 296.44. F 31.2. The list of medications was long, including an antipsychotic, Seroquel; a mood stabilizer, Lithium; and a sedative as needed, benzodiazepine. She had been abusing marijuana but had not smoked or eaten any since admittance into the hospital. After our initial intake and history, I also diagnosed her with post-traumatic stress disorder, F43.10.

I did ask what name she preferred. She did not care, but preferred Patrice. She also stated that these medications made her feel numb, and she was gaining weight.

At the time I was also teaching a graduate counseling practicum class. I gave my students this case with different demographics and ask how they would conceptualize and treat such a client. In their small groups, most of the students stated the diagnosis seemed accurate, and they would remain working with the psychiatrist with those stabilizing medications. Talk therapy, especially cognitive behavioral therapy, was a must, working on irrational cognitions.

As the semester-long class continued, our students learned more about the brain and neurocounseling, bridging brain and behavior. Understanding now that brain dysregulation often underpins many mental health and brain disorders, these same students began conceptualizing a treatment plan for Patrice in a very different manner. Talk therapy was still the foundation of counseling; however, implementing neurocounseling strategies into the plan and asking the client what her goal was became paramount. Once students better understood the brain and behaviors, these budding counselors could never go back to their traditional ways of thinking and conceptualizing treatment planning!

Neurocounseling was exactly the treatment plan that Patrice and I organized together. One goal of neurocounseling became learning emotional and physiological self-regulation and personal safety. Patrice did not like the medications or their side effects. She wanted to better understand her brain and body. She longed for skills to assist her in stability.

It was fascinating to work with Patrice on these skills, but it was also fascinating and rewarding to work with my graduate students about brain health. Therefore, the rest of this case study and chapter will discuss the treatment plan that Patrice and I developed and corresponding neuroanatomy discussions.

Patrice had quite a thorough evaluation at the hospital, so I did not want her to have to repeat assessments such as the psychosocial/medical history, but she had not completed any neurocounseling assessments. The first self-report I asked her to complete was the Neurological Dysregulation Risk Assessment (Figure 2.1).

Patrice scored "yes" on four categories. From the scoring directions, even one "yes" can indicate brain dysregulation: genetic predisposition, current diagnosis, prolonged medication use, substance or other addictions, and excessive I-technology. This self-report was not only a wonderful educational tool for Patrice, but also a treatment guide for me (see Chapter 3 for additional information). Patrice also completed an easy Symptom Checklist. This checklist served as a baseline indicator of concerns and another mechanism for goal setting (Fig 2.2). Out of 62 symptoms Patrice initially checked 31 symptoms before our counseling and neurofeedback.

In addition, I was able to offer a 19-channel electroencephalogram (EEG) to Patrice. Her 19-channel report was very helpful in customizing her treatment (Fig 2.3). Her EEG showed dysregulation and abundance of left frontal theta waves and throughout the frontal lobes; overactivation of alpha waves in the left prefrontal cortex; overactivation of low and high beta waves in the left and middle frontal cortices; and extreme overactivation at CZ in the middle of the head at 3 z scores away from the mean. In the row titled Coherence, meaning how the brainwaves

Name (or Child's Name): _____ **Age:** _____ **Date:** _____

Current Problem, Symptom or Complaint: _____

Please read each potential source of neurological dysregulation and indicate whether or not it may be a risk factor for you or your child.

	Yes	No
1. **Genetic Predisposition:** Grandparents, parents, or siblings with mental health or learning disorders (including attention deficit hyperactivity disorder), post-traumatic stress disorder, depression, generalized anxiety disorder, substance abuse, personality, or other severe psychological disorders (e.g. bipolar or schizophrenia).	___	___
2. **Pre-natal Exposure:** Maternal distress, psychotropic medication use, alcohol or substance abuse, nicotine use, or possible exposure to environmental toxins including genetically modified foods, pesticides, petrochemicals, xenestrogens in plastics, heavy metals (lead/mercury), and floride, bromine, or chlorine in water.	___	___
3. **Birth Complications:** Forcepts or vacuum delivery, oxygen loss, head injury, premature birth, difficult or prolonged labor, obstructed umbilical cord, or fetal distress.	___	___
4. **Disease and High Fever:** Sustained fever above 104 degrees due to bacterial infection, influenza, strep, meningitis, encephalitis, Reyes syndrome, or other infections or disease processes.	___	___
5. **Current Diagnosis:** Of mental health, physical health, alcohol abuse, substance abuse, or learning disorder.	___	___
6. **Poor Diet, Lack of Exercise or Sleep:** Diet high in processed food, preservatives, simple carbohydrates (sugar and flour), genetically modified foods, foods treated with herbicides, pesticides and hormones, low daily water intake, high caffeine intake, lack of adequate physical exercise (20 minutes, 5 times a week), and less than seven hours a night of sleep.	___	___

7. **Emotionally Suppressive Psychosocial Environment:** Being raised or currently living in poverty, domestic violence, physical, emotional or sexual abuse, alcoholic or mentally unstable family environment, emotional trauma, neglect, institutionalization, and inadequate maternal emotional availability or attachment.   ___   ___

8. **Mild to Severe Head Injury:** Experienced one or more blows to the head from a sports injury, fall, or auto accident (with or without loss of consciousness), or episodes of open head injury, coma, or stroke.   ___   ___

9. **Prolonged Life Distress:** Most commonly due to worry about money, work, economy, family responsibilities, relationships, personal safety, and/or health, causing sustained periods of anxiety, irritability, anger, fatigue, lack of interest, low motivation or energy, nervousness, and/or physical aches and pains.   ___   ___

10. **Stress-Related Disease:** Includes heart disease, kidney disease, hypertension, obesity, diabetes, stroke, and hormonal and/or immunological disorders.   ___   ___

11. **Prolonged Medication Use, Substance Use or Other Addictions:** Including legal or illegal drug use, substance abuse or addiction (alcohol, drugs, nicotine, caffeine, medication, gambling, sex, spending, etc.), and overuse of screen technologies (cell phones, video games, television, computers, internet, etc.).   ___   ___

12. **Seizure Disorders:** Caused by birth complications, stroke, head trauma, infection, high fever, oxygen deprivation, and/or genetic disorders and includes epilepsy, pseudo-seizures, or epileptiform seizures.   ___   ___

13. **Chronic Pain:** Related to accident, injury, or disease processes including back pain, headache and migraine pain, neck pain, facial pain, and fibromyalgia.   ___   ___

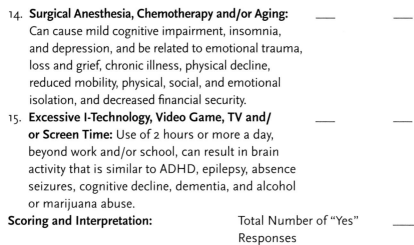

14. **Surgical Anesthesia, Chemotherapy and/or Aging:**   ____   ____
    Can cause mild cognitive impairment, insomnia,
    and depression, and be related to emotional trauma,
    loss and grief, chronic illness, physical decline,
    reduced mobility, physical, social, and emotional
    isolation, and decreased financial security.
15. **Excessive I-Technology, Video Game, TV and/**   ____   ____
    or Screen Time: Use of 2 hours or more a day,
    beyond work and/or school, can result in brain
    activity that is similar to ADHD, epilepsy, absence
    seizures, cognitive decline, dementia, and alcohol
    or marijuana abuse.

Scoring and Interpretation: Total Number of "Yes"   ____
                                           Responses

In general, the greater the number of "yes" responses, the greater the risk of significant neurological dysregulation. However, even one severe "yes" response may cause significant neurological dysregulation and result in serious mental, emotional, physical, or cognitive impairment that may benefit from further assessment and individually designed neurofeedback training.

Figure 2.1 Neurological Dysregulation Risk Assessment

Source: © Ted Chapin, Ph.D.

communicate with each other, the scan showed too much cross-talking from front to mid-back of the head. From these images, Patrice and I were able to visually better understand how and why she was behaving with manic episodes.

Not every client needs or has the resources to obtain a 19-channel EEG. For chronic clients, however, this types of report truly quantifies and assists in customizing treatment. Referring clients to board-certified neurofeedback specialists allows one more in-depth assessment to "fine-tune" treatment plans and protocols.

I combined all the results of the evaluations for Patrice to finalize the treatment plan (see Chapter 3 for more information). Seven of the symptoms that Patrice reported are often attributed to the brain location CZ, which is a part of the sensory motor strip. It was also the

Client Name: _____

Rater's Name: _____   Date: _____

Initial Assessment: (1) Place a check in the left column for any problem
that may apply.
(2) Circle the top ten.
(3) Place an asterisk after the top three.

Every Ten Sessions: Please rate changes since beginning NFB in the right
column, using scale below.

S = Same   I = Improved   M = Much Improved   NA = Not Applicable

CZ

__ __ Difficulty Visual Recognition
of Objects or Words
__ __ Retention of Information
__ __ Short-Term Memory
__ __ Foggy Thinking
__ __ Poor Reading Comprehension
__ __ Tired When Reading or Problem
Solving
__ __ Mental Sluggishness
__ __ Hyperactive, Restlessness,
Can't Sit Still
__ __ Unable to Quiet
or Calm My Body
__ __ Falling Asleep
__ __ Headaches
__ __ Managing/Coping
with Chronic Pain
__ __ Tics, Body Tremors,
Involuntary Muscle Spasms
__ __ Seizures with a Motor
Component
__ __ Talkativeness

F4

__ __ Easily Annoyed or Irritated
__ __ Anxious Mood
__ __ Easily Angered
__ __ Impulsive
__ __ Emotionally Volatile/
Explosive
__ __ Oppositional or Defiant
__ __ Indifferent/Unresponsive to
Others
__ __ Restricted Emotional
Expression
__ __ Developmental Delay/
Socially Awkward

F3/F4

__ __ Inattention, Day Dreaming,
Distracted
__ __ Disorganized, Poor Planning
and Sequencing
__ __ Sustaining Focus or Staying
on Task

O1

__ __ Emotional Trauma or Traumatic
         Stress

__ __ Poor Quality Sleep

__ __ Preoccupation with Artistic
         Interests or Skills

__ __ Easily Tired or Fatigued

__ __ Frequently Ill

__ __ Easily Frightened

__ __ Staying Asleep or Disturbed
         Sleep

__ __ Lack of Dreaming or Nightmares

__ __ Racing Thoughts or Anxiety

__ __ Insufficient Self-Soothing

__ __ Self-Medicating (Alcohol,
         Drugs, Food)

__ __ Cognitive Inefficiency
         or Difficulty Thinking

F3

__ __ Unhappy

__ __ Feeling Worthless

__ __ Little to Look Forward To

__ __ Negative Self-Talk

__ __ Depressed Mood

__ __ Poor Retrieval of Information

__ __ Lack of Energy, Motivation,
         Interest

__ __ Fibromyalgia/ Chronic Fatigue

FZ

__ __ Stubborn, "My Way or the
         Highway"

__ __ Maintaining Concentration

__ __ Forgetfulness

__ __ Fretting or Excessive Worry

__ __ Compulsive, Repetitive
         Behaviors

__ __ Obsessive, Annoying
         Thoughts

__ __ Excessive Passiveness

__ __ Too Pleasing, Open-minded,
         Conciliatory

__ __ Can't Let Things Go

__ __ Stuck on the Negative

__ __ Age Related Cognitive/
         Memory Problems

__ __ Extremely Focused Interests
         or Rigid Behavior

__ __ Preoccupation with Pain

__ __ Busy Thoughts Causing
         Disrupted Sleep

__ __ Marked Learning or
         Cognitive Deficits

Figure 2.2 Problem Checklist and Symptom Rating Form

Source: Adapted from Paul Swingle Clinical Q. © Ted Chapin, Ph.D.

highest overactivated portion of her EEG. I knew to start talk therapy and neurofeedback, if possible, at CZ, located right in the middle of the head between the ears.

Talk therapy focused on basic biofeedback and neurocounseling tools to immediately assist in calming down the sympathetic nervous system.

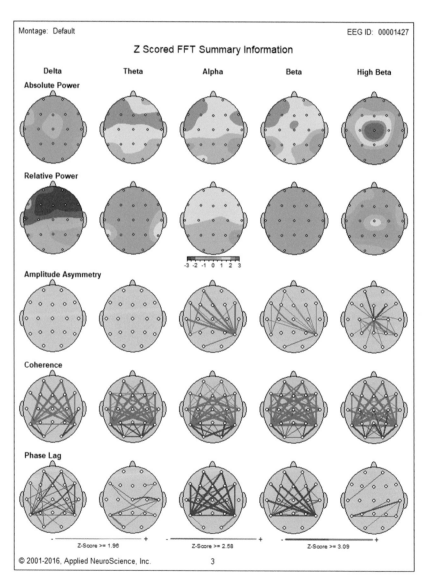

Figure 2.3 EEG

Patrice worked on diaphragmatic breathing, skin temperature control, and heart rate variability (HRV). All of my clients are given a small hand-held thermometer to practice with at home. Her baseline peripheral skin temperature went from 85 degrees to a consistent 92 degrees. Ninety-one degrees is often needed for peak performance and focused attention. Patrice purchased a smart-phone version of HRV called Inner Balance that she used to practice daily.

In talk therapy, we worked on therapeutic lifestyle changes such as sleep hygiene, eating well, and exercising daily for at least 20 minutes per day (Ivey, Ivey & Zalaquett, 2014). Patrice took the How Healthy is Your Lifestyle Inventory. She had high scores on five items, and low scores on the remaining inventory. These scores helped us add more goals to our overall treatment. We had several conjoint counseling sessions with her mom, setting boundaries and limits for both of them (Fig 2.4).

Her self-reports of symptoms were gradually lessening, but her flat affect remained. We began working with the psychiatrist, but he needed to see at least one month of stabile functioning before weaning Patrice off any medications.

Patrice wanted to engage in neurofeedback. Her 19-channel results and other self-reports offered us the opportunity to customize her neurofeedback (NFB) treatment plans with specific protocols to work on those dysregulated brain locations. As mentioned, we began the first five NFB sessions working on the sensory motor rhythm at 12–15 hertz, calming down her central nervous system. I reinforced low beta and inhibited high alpha and theta brainwaves.

Much like the information in the next few chapters using LORETA brain images and specific neurocounseling interventions for targeted areas of dysregulation, for Patrice we followed her own symptom check-list concerns, self-reports, and QEEGs to continue working on her needs. Patrice was able to complete 20 sessions of NFB. We began conducting NFB twice per week for 20-minute sessions each time. We were able to combine our talk therapy with the NFB sessions, joining the best of both worlds. Based upon our session, I would ask Patrice to work on a home-work assignment between our sessions. The homework might be practicing skin temperature or just diaphragmatic breathing.

In one of her later sessions, Patrice was watching the movie, *The DaVinci Code* during NFB. We were working on the midline of the brain at FZ to PZ

HOW HEALTHY IS YOUR LIFESTYLE?

Name _____ Gender _____ Age _____
Race/Ethnicity _____ Date _____

Circle your response

ALIOSTRESS/EUSTRESS/STRESS LEVELS: What is your level of stress?

1	2	3	4	5	1	2	3	4	5
Eustress, life is generally calm and interesting, few major or minor stressors, recover from stress fairly quickly. Pleasant, happy life.	Manageable, stressors can be troublesome, but recover. Some tough stressors time to time. Life is good.	Often feel stressed, sometimes for days, lose some sleep, old stressful events often with me. However, generally life is good.	Constant feeling of stress, pressure, sleep problems, old events still with me. Can blow up, but manage. Life is OK, but	Chronic stress, tired, angry, sleep difficulties, feel sad, easy to blow up, fall apart, out of control. Need to change my life.					

1. Exercise: How frequently do you exercise (walk, swim, bike, garden, run, rock climb)?

1	2	3	4	5	1	2	3	4	5
5–7 days weekly	4–5 days weekly	2–3 times weekly	Occasional	Couch potato					

2. Nutrition: What is your typical diet?

1	2	3	4 (S.A.D)	5	1	2	3	4	5
Vegan, vegetarian, fish	Low fat, lean meat, fruit, vegetables	Mediterranean, Paleo	Stn. Amer. Diet	Fast food, fries, sugar					

3. Sleep: How many hours nightly, including how restful is your sleep?

1	2	3	4	5	1	2	3	4	5
7–9 hours	7 hours	Sleep challenges	Many meds	Serious difficulty					

4. Social relations: How connected are you to others—close relationships, family, friends, groups?

1	2	3	4	5	1	2	3	4	5
Well-connected	Connected	Friends, some groups	Somewhat social	Alone, angry, sad					

4a. Intimacy, Sex Life: How satisfied are you with your sex life?

1	2	3	4	5	1	2	3	4	5
Highly	Moderately	Somewhat	Dissatisfied	Do not care					

5. Cognitive Challenge: How actively do you involve yourself in mind-expanding cognitive challenges?

1	2	3	4	5	1	2	3	4	5
Joy in constantly learning, searching for the New	Involved, active	Moderately interested, read some books, puzzles	Some, no more than 3 hours a week	None					

6. Cultural Health and Cultural Identity: Awareness of cultural issues influencing, you, including sense of cultural identity.

1	2	3	4	5	1	2	3	4	5
Empathy for self and others. See self-in-relation, race/ethnicity, etc. awareness, life vision	At least two of the preceding plus life vision	One of the preceding, some life vision	Slightly aware of issues	Oppressive, no real life vision					

7. Meditation, Yoga, etc.: How often do you engage in this practice?

1	2	3	4	5		1	2	3	4	5
Daily	3–4 times weekly	Aware, occasional	Absent	Hyper, cannot do						

8. Drugs, Alcohol: Use of alcohol or other drugs?

1	2	3	4	5		1	2	3	4	5
None	Moderate	Has become part of life	Become a focus	Addicted						

9. Medication and Supplements: How aware are you of possible issues plus appropriate contact with physicians?

1	2	3	4	5		1	2	3	4	5
Regular contact with physician, follow directions	Frequent contact	Occasional, some difficulty following directions	Seldom	Never						

10. Positive thinking/optimism/happiness: Do you have resilient positive attitudes and a good level of happiness?

1	2	3	4	5
Resilient, positive, optimistic	Most of the time	Usually, not always	Seldom	Infrequent

1	2	3	4	5

11. Belief, Values: How engaged are you with living a meaningful life?

1	2	3	4	5
A life center	Involved	Occasional involvement	Never	Not interested

1	2	3	4	5

11a. Spirituality, Religiosity: Do you participate in spiritual or religious activities?

1	2	3	4	5
Daily	Between 2–4 days a week	Once a week	Holidays only	Do not believe

1	2	3	4	5

12. Nature/Green/Garden: How often you engage in outside/nature activities?

1	2	3	4	5	1	2	3	4	5
Gets outdoors often	Frequent	Sometimes	Seldom	Almost never					

13. Smoking: Do you smoke? If yes, how much?

1	2	3	4	5	1	2	3	4	5
Never	Never, but exposed to secondary	Stopped smoking	Try to stop	Still smoking					

14. Screen time (TV, Cell, iPad, Computer): Amount of time in front of a screen?

1	2	3	4	5	1	2	3	4	5
None	2 hours or less daily	4 hours daily	6 or more hours daily	Never off-line					

15. Relaxation and Having Fun: How frequently are you involved in leisure or relaxation activities?

1	2	3	4	5		1	2	3	4	5
Something every day	5–6 hours weekly	3–4 hours weekly	Limited and stressed	Workaholic/ stressed out						

16. Education: What level of education have you completed?

1	2	3	4	5		1	2	3	4	5
College, serious hobby	College	Comm. College	High school/ GED	Drop out						

17. Money and Privilege: What is your financial situation? Do you benefit from privilege because of race or other factor?

1	2	3	4	5		1	2	3	4	5
Have it all, privileged	Comfortable	Making it	On edge, but OK	Poor, oppressed						

18. Helping others/community involvement/social justice action: How frequently you help others or your community?

1	2	3	4	5		1	2	3	4	5
Daily action	Weekly action	Often involved	No time	Destructive						

19. Art, Music, Dance, Literature: How frequently do you release your artistic abilities?

1	2	3	4	5		1	2	3	4	5
Daily	Several times weekly	Moderate/frequent	Occasional	None						

20. Joy, Humor, Zest for Living, Keeping it Simple, Not Overdoing: How happy or how much fun do you have?

1	2	3	4	5		1	2	3	4	5
Life is a blast	Fun most of the time	Moderately happy	Now and then	Never						

SELF-EVALUATION OF GENERAL LIFESTYLE

Work: What is the level of your work or retirement activities?

1	2	3	4	5		1	2	3	4	5
Fully employed. Retired, never bored	Partial employment. Retired and active	Temporary work. OK, but sometimes bored	Jobless. Bored, less happy	Given up work. Inactive, depressed						

In Control: How much in control of your life are you?

1	2	3	4	5		1	2	3	4	5
In full control of my life	Mostly in control	Somewhat in control	Low control	Out of control						

Health: How healthy are you?

1	2	3	4	5		1	2	3	4	5
Very healthy	Occasional issues	Good, but could be better	Major issues	Very poor						

Stability: How stable is your life currently?

1	2	3	4	5		1	2	3	4	5
Highly stable	Moderately	Some ups and downs	Unstable	Chaotic						

Resilience: Your ability to bounce back from life challenges

1	2	3	4	5		1	2	3	4	5
Back "at it" soon	Temporarily troubled	Worry a fair amount	Difficult, but do it	Overwhelmed						

Satisfaction: How satisfied are you with your current lifestyle?

1	2	3	4	5		1	2	3	4	5
Highly	Moderately	Somewhat	Dissatisfied	Helpless						

Action: How ready are you to make changes to increase your wellbeing?

1	2	3	4	5		1	2	3	4	5
Ready to change	Want to change	Thinking about it	Some interest	Not interested						

Figure 2.4 How Healthy is Your Lifestyle Inventory
Source: Allen Ivey, Mary Bradford Ivey, and Carlos Zalaquett © 2014

(refer to Chapter 5 in your text) using a theta, alpha, and gamma (TAG) synchrony training. I noticed from the EEG recording that the alpha and theta waves were working together. At that point we know that the front of her head is communicating with the back of the head at PZ. This is called coherence, so I stopped the movie and asked her what she was feeling. She calmly stated, "Relaxed and empowered by the strong female detective." I jotted the words down in her notes, and we continued on with the rest of the session. These words helped me know what kind of homework was needed until we saw each other again. When Patrice left, I reminded her that whenever she felt frustrated to find that relaxed and empowered state again.

After 10 NFB sessions, Patrice did another Symptom Checklist, noting those symptoms/behaviors that had "Stayed the Same, Improved or Much Improved." Patrice checked that 5 out of the 31 symptoms had improved since beginning counseling three months before.

After our eleventh session, Patrice secured a job that only allowed NFB sessions to occur once per week instead of two. Although that was not our preference, the research (Thompson & Thompson, 2015) shows that NFB creates neuroplasticity, and the improvements will stay the same unless additional dysregulation occurs. We were diligent in meeting once per week for the remainder of our time together.

At the end of 20 NFB sessions, Patrice and her mom wanted a post-19-channel EEG conducted. Her results were remarkable, qualitatively and quantitatively. Again, for all the data from Patrice, we could customize the next 20 sessions based upon her needs. At the end of her 20 sessions another Symptom Checklist was taken. This time Patrice reported all 31 symptoms had improved. During our last meeting, she stated she was feeling relaxed yet focused. A final QEEG was requested, but our scheduled appointment occurred during the COVID-19 pandemic shutdown. Patrice reports today from a telephone call that she is functioning well and off all medications. She continues to exercise daily, eat well, and maintain healthy sleep hygiene.

Neuroanatomy and Brainwaves

In Section 2 of this book, the reader will have specific definitions of brain locations and functions within each chapter using the Head

Map of Functions illustration. Before reading those neurocounseling interventions, here is the psychoeducational neuroanatomy information that was shared with Patrice and most of our clients.

Understanding just some very basic and foundational information about the brain and body is all that is necessary. A few clients will ask for more depth, and that information is happily supplied. In this chapter, first a fun teaching brain quiz will be offered, and then a more in-depth journey will be discussed.

I created a true/false Brain Quiz to help explain the basics. Take the quiz (Fig 2.5). Then each answer will be discussed. The information offered below has been taken from three main sources (Russell-Chapin, 2020; Field, Jones & Russell-Chapin, 2017; and Chapin & Russell-Chapin, 2014). Please refer to any of these three books for further elaboration about the brain and body.

Here are the answers to the Brain Quiz with more information about each question that may assist you with your clients.

1. The adult human brain weighs approximately 4 pounds.
2. Our lifestyle impacts the efficiency of the brain.
3. There are approximately 300 million neurons that can fire in the brain.
4. The human brain is fully developed by age four.
5. The brain is a plastic and malleable organ.
6. When parents say to an adolescent, "What were you thinking?," there is a reasonable explanation for the poor decision!
7. Physical exercise is one of the major factors in brain growth.
8. Most of our serotonin is produced in the brain.
9. Persons over 65 years of age are not able to create new neuronal pathways.
10. Our brains tend to function over-aroused, under-aroused, or unstable.
11. The brain cannot be taught to self-regulate itself.
12. Alpha waves are the electrical brain frequencies that keep you alert in this lecture.
13. Neurotherapy/neurofeedback has not been scientifically proven as an effective treatment modality for brain dysfunction.
14. We only use about 10% of the brain.

Figure 2.5 The Brain Quiz: True or False
Source: Lori Russell-Chapin

Brain Quiz Answers

1. The adult human brain weighs approximately 4 pounds. False
    The human brain typically weighs 3 pounds. If your two fists are placed together, that is about the correct size and shape. The brain has a gelatinous texture and consists mostly of water, fat, and protein. It uses a lot of energy to function well, requiring about 20% of the body's oxygen and 25% of the body's glucose.

2. Our lifestyle impacts the efficiency of the brain. True
    A valid and reliable brain takes in information very rapidly and correctly. This requires the brain and body to be healthy and communicate with all aspects of the brain and the body. How lives are lived is extremely important, so the more engaged and active a person is the better. Taking a wellness approach to living is the best, from proper nutrition to sleep hygiene to mental and physical exercise.

3. There are approximately 300 million neurons that fire in the brain. False
    There are approximately 86 billion neurons firing in the brain. Each of these neurons connect to 10,000 other synapses, resulting in over 86,000 trillion synaptic connections! Our brains are quite remarkable.

4. The human brain is fully developed by age four. False
    For years this was the accepted theory, but through research we now believe that the brain reaches full maturity in the late twenties.

5. The brain is a plastic and malleable organ. True
    The brain entrains to everything around it from noise to chaos to order. It is plastic and has the capacity to grow new neuronal pathways in both the negative and positive directions. Negative plasticity is found in destructive behaviors and addictions. Positive plasticity is demonstrated in constructive behaviors such as learning a new language.

6. When parents say to an adolescent who made a mistake, "What were you thinking?," there is a reasonable explanation for their behaviors. True
    The brain develops from the back to the front of the head. The pre-frontal cortex is the last to mature, so often the adolescent brain does take more risks and makes poorer choices.

7. Physical exercise is one of the major factors in brain growth. True
    Physical exercise helps the brain and body to continue to function well. At least 20 minutes a day of aerobic exercise with one minute

of raising the heart rate is often recommended. Exercise elicits brain-derived neurotropic factors (BDNF) that alert the body to wake up and learn from the insulin hormone to the cardiac hormone. Strength training also keeps the bones healthy and telomeres intact.

8. Most of our serotonin is produced in the brain. False

Most serotonin is produced in the gut. Our microbiota-gut-brain axis is critical to our overall health. This enteric nervous system has over 600 neurons associated with its functioning. What we eat does matter, and the gut has been associated with many mental health concerns.

9. Persons over the age of 65 are not able to create new neuronal pathways. False

The brain needs and wants to be challenged with healthy activities. The brain loves to learn new tasks and skills. At any age we can continue to learn, grow, and develop new neuronal pathways. Of course, a healthy and engaged lifestyle plays an essential role in this growth, especially in the older population.

10. Our brain tends to function over-aroused, under-aroused, or unstable. True

Often because we do live life, our brains become dysregulated. In the beginning of Chapter 2 we discussed the variety of causes for dysregulation with the Neurological Dysregulation Risk Assessment. When the brain is dysregulated, and depending on where the dysregulation occurs in the brain, the brain may be over-aroused producing behaviors such as anxiety and agitation. Under-arousal in certain brain locations may bring about such behavioral changes as depression and lethargy. The unstable brain may have difficulty changing from one brainwave state to another, so behaviors such as bipolar and insomnia may occur.

11. The brain cannot be taught to self-regulate itself. False

When healthy, the brain is a self-regulating organ. We can help the brain learn to self-regulate again through our lifestyle and practicing skills daily that help us stay calm and focused, such as diaphragmatic breathing, skin temperature, and heart rate variability. Neurofeedback and neurocounseling skills also assist in teaching the brain to re-regulate.

12. Alpha brainwaves are the electrical frequencies that keep you alert when reading this material. False

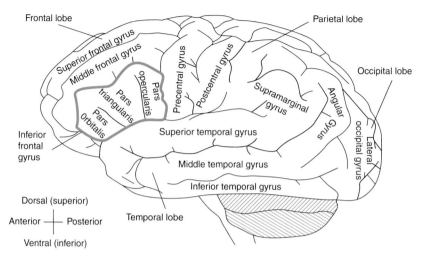

Figure 2.6 Brainwaves and their functions

Understanding some aspects of brainwaves is important for counselors and clients.

Figure 2.6 illustrates the actual brainwaves and their functions. The brainwaves often even look like many of their corresponding behaviors. For example, delta waves are slower than beta waves, thus expecting a slow wave to produce a slower behavior such as sleep. The correct answer for this question would be that low beta waves around 13–15 hertz would keep you alert and focused for reading. To remember the brainwave categories, the mnemonic Do Think About Brain Growth may help: D stands for delta, T stands for theta, A represents alpha, B represents beta, and G stands for gamma. There are other brainwaves, but these are the major categories (Chapin & Russell-Chapin, 2014).

13. Neurofeedback has not been scientifically proven as an effective treatment modality for brain dysfunction. False

Neurofeedback (NFB) has efficacy ratings for treatment effectiveness. NFB has been found efficacious for many treatment disorders especially attention deficit hyperactivity disorder (ADHD).

14. We only use 10% of the brain. False

This is a myth that has been around for many years. We all utilize 100% of the brain; however, the level of dysregulation makes the brain less effective. Helping clients learn self-regulation skills makes the brain more organized and efficient.

A More Comprehensive Look at the Brain

Thompson & Thompson (2003) in *The Neurofeedback Book*, Kershaw & Wade (2011) in *Brain Change Therapy*, Chapin & Russell-Chapin (2014), Jones (2017), and Russell-Chapin (2020) all offer descriptive and concise reviews of the brain and basic neuroanatomy. The following materials are a composite of their work. The next few pages will be a general review and focus on the brain's major structures and functions.

Brain Structures and Functions

These will also be featured in Section 2 showcasing each of the 19 brain locations. For this discussion, though, a general description of the basic brain will be offered. The brain can be divided into three major regions: the forebrain, the midbrain, and the hindbrain. The forebrain is the seat of higher reasoning or our executive functions. Another name may be the neocortex. The midbrain controls emotion and motivation and involves the limbic system. The hindbrain, the reptilian brain, is where our survival instinct and autonomic functions originate. This three-part model is called the triune (three-in-one) brain (Chapin & Russell-Chapin, 2014; Russell-Chapin, 2020).

Forebrain

The forebrain consists of the thalamus, hypothalamus, and cerebrum. The cerebrum includes the cerebral cortex and basal ganglia and connects to the limbic system. The largest part of the brain is responsible for communication between the midbrain and the cerebral cortex. It is the hypothalamus, along with the pituitary gland, that controls the endocrine (hormonal) activity in the body. This maintains homeostasis (heart rate, vasoconstriction, temperature, blood pressure, digestion, body weight, etc.). The forebrain also directs such complex behaviors as social interaction, learning, working memory, speech, language, and habit control.

Hindbrain

The hindbrain consists of the brainstem, the cerebellum, the medulla oblongata or upper spinal cord, and the pons. It is responsible for innervation to the face and neck, heart and lung regulation, skeletal muscle tone, coordination and precise motor performance, working memory, sleep, and arousal. The hindbrain is essential to maintaining consciousness.

Midbrain

The midbrain or limbic system consists of the amygdala, the thalamus, and the hippocampus. The amygdala connects all areas of emotion, the autonomic nervous system, the endocrine system, and unconscious memory. The amygdala can be stimulated by a triggering event and is related to post-traumatic stress disorder. The thalamus routes all sensory information except smell through the respective visual, auditory, somatosensory, and motor cortexes. It is also important in electroencephalography (EEG) (electrical) rhythms and provides a feedback loop with the cortex. The hippocampus also has connections to areas related to emotion, the autonomic nervous system, and the endocrine system, involving consciousness, laying down of memory, and recall. The hippocampus helps to compare present situations with past memories.

Cerebral Cortex

The cerebral cortex or the outer portion of the brain integrates information from the sense organs, manages emotions, retains memory, and mediates thinking and emotional expression. It is divided into two hemispheres, the right and left, and is connected by the corpus callosum or neuronal fibers allowing communication between the hemispheres. Short fibers act as major roads connecting areas of the right and left hemisphere and long fibers act as superhighways allowing fast connection between areas. The corpus collosum has the biggest collection of nerve fibers in the entire nervous system, with over 200 million interhemispheric connections (Luders, Thompson & Toga, 2010).

Cingulate Gyrus

At the front of the corpus collosum is the cingulate gyrus. It is active in cognitive tasks, maintaining focus, and problem solving. Problems with the cingulate gyrus involve obsessive thinking and compulsive behavior.

Right Hemisphere

The right hemisphere is generally involved with social interaction, spontaneity, and aesthetic appreciation. More specifically, the right hemisphere helps to regulate attention, inhibit old habits, and sense the gestalt of an experience. It involves parallel processing, spatial relationships, the understanding of geometric forms, orientation in space, and holistic perception. It also plays a vital role in the emotional aspects of language through the processing of verbal intonation. Right-hemisphere dominance is noted by distractibility, stimulus seeking, novelty, change, emotional involvement, extroversion, and an external locus of control. The right hemisphere is related to histrionic tendencies, impulsiveness, and mania. It relies on an accommodating, fast, and simultaneous style of information processing. Its dominant neurotransmitters are noradrenaline (speeding up action) and serotonin (slowing down action). Right-hemisphere dominance is used for emotional processing and can be a source of problems with impulsivity, aggression, disinhibition, anxiety, and social interaction.

Left Hemisphere

The left hemisphere is involved with language, writing, math, logical reasoning, and analytical, sequential processing. More specifically, it is the center for speech and syntax, writing, auditory verbal representation, object naming, word recall, visual imaging by auditory input, letter and word perception and recognition, abstract verbal formation, and perception of complex relationships. It also regulates attention, aids in inhibiting action and switching our responses, and is the source of inner dialogue used to regulate behavior. Left-hemisphere dominance is noted by a lack of emotions, introversion, goal-directed thinking and action, and an internal locus of control. It relies on an assimilative, slower style of serial processing. Its dominant neurotransmitter is dopamine (responsible for reward-driven behavior). Left-hemisphere dominance is what is typically measured on an intelligence test and can be the source of problems with language, dyslexia, learning disorders, negative internal dialogue, and depression.

Brain Lobes

FRONTAL LOBES

Each hemisphere is divided into four lobes. These are the frontal, temporal, parietal, and occipital lobes. The frontal lobes are responsible for executive functions, thus helping plan for the future, anticipate consequences, analyze choices, learn and express language (Broca's area), and inhibit inappropriate or unwanted behavior. The frontal lobes house personality, sense of self-confidence, independent judgment, willingness to take risks, and our extroverted or introverted nature. Persons with attention deficit hyperactivity disorder often have problems with their frontal lobes. Problems with the right frontal lobe often result in anxiety. Problems with the left, result in depression.

TEMPORAL LOBES

The temporal lobes assist with auditory processing, short-term or working memory, comprehension of word meaning (Wernicke area), and integration of new information, retrieval of words, and the emotional valance of thoughts and behavior including temper control. The temporal lobes organize our sense of hearing and smell. Problems with the left temporal lobe can involve aggression, violent thoughts, sensitivity to provocation, paranoia, decreased verbal memory, and emotional instability. Problems with the right temporal lobe can involve perception of melodies, meaning of verbal tone, social cues, and facial expression. The temporal lobes involve social difficulty, problems processing music, distortion in visual and auditory memory, a sense of déjà vu, and religious or moral preoccupation.

PARIETAL LOBES

The parietal lobes are involved in integrating raw sensory information, perception of the physical body, and motor functions including touch, pressure, temperature, taste, pain, spatial relations, and navigation.

Problems with the parietal lobes include difficulty processing information, understanding directions, sensory sensitivity, physiological arousal, attention, and hypervigilance.

OCCIPITAL LOBE

The occipital lobe is responsible for visual processing, image construction, visual memory, and pattern recognition. Problems with the occipital lobe can involve impaired vision and difficulty dreaming. The occipital lobe has also been implicated in problems with post-traumatic stress disorder.

Neurobiology

For years, it was believed that the brain had about 100 billion neurons. Research from Dr. Suzana Herculano-Houzel discovered that there may only be 87 billion neurons in the brain. That still is an amazing number, but how dense the neurons are is very important too. Through a process called "brain soup," these researchers took brain tissue and placed the tissue first in formaldehyde to stabilize it. Then the tissue was dissolved into a grainy soup where the nuclei could be easily counted (Herculano-Houzel, 2016). The brain's 87 billion neurons receive and send information through electrochemical communication. Every neuron is composed of a nucleus, axon, and dendrites. The synaptic space between dendrites and other neurons is filled with neurotransmitters. Neurotranmitters facilitate neuronal communication. A process called methylation is responsible for "turning on" or "turning off" specific neurotransmitter production. Food supplements such as niacin and folic acid are sometimes used to increase or decrease the methylation process of targeted neurotransmitters. Communication between neurons occurs when chemical ions in one axon generate an electrical charge that is sent to the dendrites of another. As sequences of neurons fire or stop firing across the synaptic gap, the function related to that part of the brain is activated or inhibited. Learning occurs when a specific circuit reacts in a certain pattern. This allows a memory to form or an action to be re-experienced.

A neuron's resting electrical potential is roughly 70 millivolts. This is a measure of the difference of the charge of the ions inside the cell and those outside it when the neuron is not firing (Fisch, 1999). To fire, a neuron must become depolarized at about −55 millivolts, creating an action potential or release of neurotransmitters and electrical activity. When polarized, no firing occurs. When hyperpolarized, the neurons become dull and less responsive to other cells. Millions of neurons firing together produces patterns of electrical activity called brainwaves. Sterman (1995) suggested that the thalamus was the source of cortical potentials measured on the scalp and responsible for the generation of particular brainwave patterns. The major brainwave patterns are delta, theta, alpha, beta, and gamma. Remember that the brainwaves correlate to similar behaviors. Low, slow waves often are associated with behaviors such as sleep and meditation. High, fast waves are often depicted with behaviors such as problem-solving and even anxiety.

Brainwave Bandwidths

Delta is 1–4 Hertz (Hz) or cycles per minute and is related to hypothalamic function and deep, dreamless sleep. Persons with ADHD have higher delta waves when awake. They are also related to dementia and head injury. Theta is 4–7 Hz and is produced in the limbic system and related to twilight states of drowsiness, meditation, hypnosis, past memory, and symbolic imagery. Those with ADHD have been found to have intrusive theta waves when trying to concentrate. Theta waves are also important in healing and recovery. Alpha is 8–12 Hz and is related to thalamic function and focused relaxation. Alpha is thought to be the brain's idling rhythm. Strong alpha waves are important to health, a key to weight management, and the focus of peak sports performance. With age, alpha tends to decrease. Once it disappears, death will soon follow. Beta is 12–40 Hz. Lower beta brainwaves are active in concentration, sequential thinking, and problem solving. Higher beta waves are related to anxiety, irritability, and negative internal chatter. Lower beta waves are related to depression. Gamma waves range from 25 to 100 Hz but are usually thought to be around 40 Hz. They are related to cognitive efficiency, rapid eye movement in sleep, and deep states of meditative compassion. Persons with learning disabilities have lower gamma waves.

Brain Electrical Activity

The electrical activity of the brain is very important, and because it is related to various psychological and behavioral problems, its healthy

Electroencephalography 0.16–45.0 Hz	The EEG is composed of many electrical frequencies produced by the cortex and driving mechanisms. The EEG is most commonly measured from 0.16 to 45.0 Hz or similar range of frequencies.	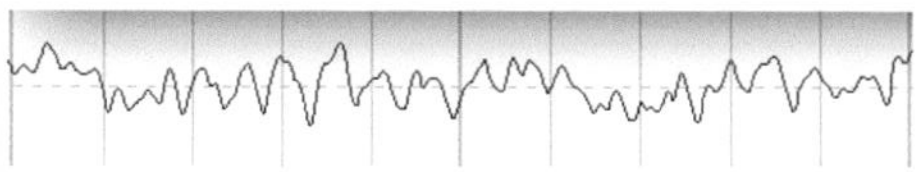
Delta 0.5–3.5 Hz	The delta frequencies are predominant during sleep and recovery in healthy adults.	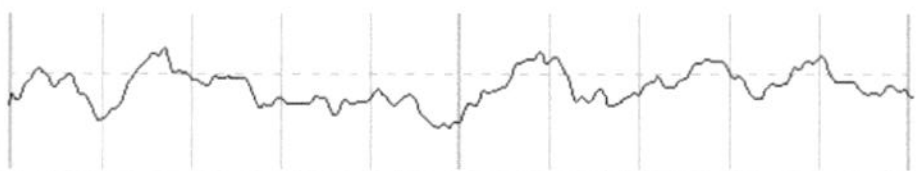
Theta 4.0–7.7 Hz	The theta frequencies are predominant during drowsing or are associated with creative states.	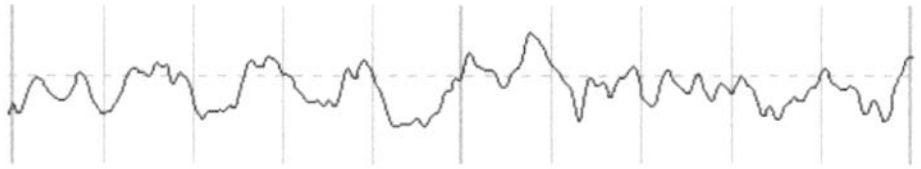
Alpha 8.0–12.0 Hz	The alpha frequencies are predominant during an awake and alert state yet not during cortical arousal. They are often referred to as the idle rhythm.	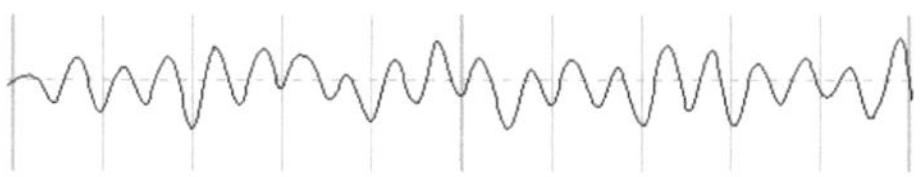
Low Beta 13.0–21.0 Hz	The lower beta frequencies are present during times of focus and engagement.	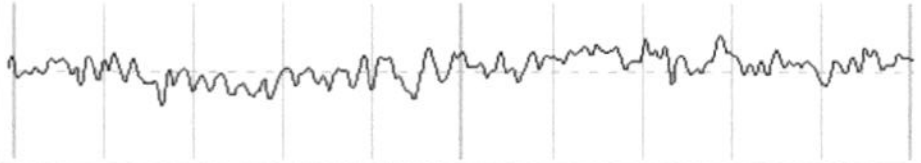
High Beta 22.0–35.0 Hz	The higher beta frequencies are predominant during concentration and higher levels of cortical activation.	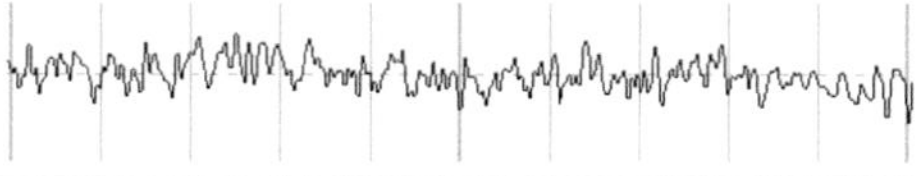
Gamma 35.0–45.0 Hz	The gamma frequencies represent higher levels of cognition and are often representative of learning processes.	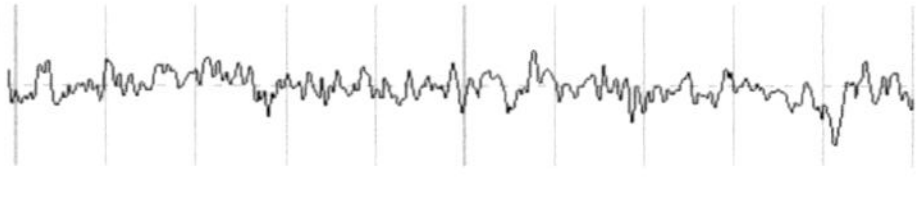

Figure 2.7 EEG frequency band ranges, description and morphology
All EEG samples are filtered at 16–45 Hz. Gain = 70uV. Time = 2 seconds.
Source: Permission granted by Leslie Sherlin, 2020.

regulation is essential. There are many factors that can cause dysregulation of the brain's electrical activity from just living life to abuse of drugs and alcohol to high fevers to genetic predispositions to brain injury.

The brain's neuronal communication occurs in discernible patterns based upon the connections between structures and the type of gray or white matter found in the cerebral cortex. Gray matter refers to neuronal cell bodies that have unmyelinated axons, dendrites, and glial cells. Glial cells provide nutritional and structural support for the brain's blood-brain barrier. Unmyelinated neurons are slower moving. White matter refers to areas that contain mainly myelinated or fiber-sheath-protected axons. Myelination gives this matter its white color. The less dense, myelinated axons create the "superhighways" that allow high-speed transmission of signals from one structure to another and from one region of the brain to another. These communication patterns occur in many different patterns, from front to back, hemisphere to hemisphere and within hemispheres. Myelination is greater in the right hemisphere, due to its long-distance, emotion-based communication functions. The left hemisphere relies on more sequential organization and has less myelination. Note that the myelination of the neurons is not complete until the second decade of life. This is why teenagers have less developed executive functions. It is also important to understand that many experts now believe that most brain illnesses result from lack of communication or coherence between brain regions whether that be local, regional, and/or global.

Neurons

Two types of neurons are important for emotional well-being. They are mirror neurons and spindle neurons. Mirror neurons fire when performing an action or when watching someone else perform an action. They are thought to be a form of imitative learning and are important in interpersonal empathy and perhaps the transmission of cultural values and emotional expression (Iacoboni, 2008). Spindle neurons are unusually large neurons with only one dendrite that transmits signals from region to region across the brain. They appear to be important for emotional communication, social emotions, and moral sense (Allman et al., 2001).

Neuronal functioning directly affects the brain's ability to communicate and self-regulate. Problems with neurotransmitters have

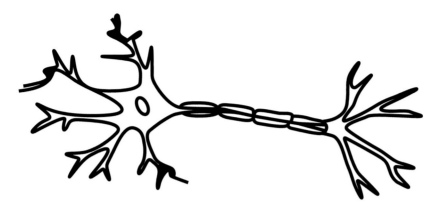

Figure 2.8 Neurons

been found to affect mood, cognition, and interpersonal interaction. Mirror neurons have been implicated in autism spectrum disorders and spindle neurons in psychotic disorders. Medication treatment, developed to help restore the brain's healthy self-regulation, has been found to have limited efficacy and unwanted side effects. This has motivated many clients and therapists to search for alternative strategies. Neurofeedback, focusing on the brain's electrical activity, is one such option.

Of course, there is so much more material that we can share with our clients. Again, typically clients will let you know how much information they need or want. In the Case of Patrice, an undergraduate degree in health sciences made her eager for as much information as possible, especially when it was related to her issues and could be applied in daily living.

Conclusions

In Chapter 2 the Case of Patrice was presented to assist the reader in seeing how neurocounseling can be integrated into our regular talk therapy sessions. Teaching clients basic neuroanatomy and neuroscience information offers a better understanding of how and why certain skills are utilized. Neurofeedback was also discussed and implemented as a possible quantitative tool.

References

Allman, J., Atiya, H., Erewin, E., Nimchinsky, P. & Hof, A. (2001). Anterior cingulated cortex: The evolution of an interface between emotion and cognition. *Annals of the New York Academy of Sciences* 935, 107–117.

Chapin, T.J. & Russell-Chapin, L.A. (2014). *Neurotherapy and Neurofeedback: Based-based treatment for psychological and behavioral problems*. New York: Routledge.

Field, T.A., Jones, L.K. & Russell-Chapin, L.A. (2017). *Neurocounseling: Brain-based approaches*. Alexandria, VA: American Counseling Association.

Fisch, B.J. (1999). *Fisch and Spehlmann's EEG Primer: Basic principles of digital and analog EEG*. Amsterdam and New York: Elsevier.

Herculano-Houzel, S. (2016). *The Human Advantage: A new understanding of how our brain became remarkable*. Cambridge, MA: The MIT Press.

Iacoboni, M. (ed.) (2008). *Mirroring People: The new science of how we connect with others*. New York: Farrar, Straus & Giroux.

Ivey, A.E., Ivey, M.B. & Zalaquett, C. (2014). Therapeutic Lifestyle Change Inventory.

Jones, L.K. (2017). Anatomy and brain development. In Fields, T., Jones, L. & Russell-Chapin, L.A. (eds.) *Neurocounseling: Brain-based approaches*. Alexandria, VA: American Counseling Association.

Kershaw, C.J. & Wade, J.W. (2011). *Brain Change Therapy*. New York: Norton.

Luders, E., Thompson, P.M. & Toga, A.W. (2010). The development of the corpus collosum in the healthy human brain. *Journal of Neuroscience* 30, 10985–10990.

Russell-Chapin, L.A. (2020). Basic concepts of neuroscience in counseling and counselor education. In Mary Olufunmilayo Adekson (ed.) *Handbook of Counseling and Counselor Education*. New York: Routledge.

Sherlin, L. (2020). Personal communication.

Sterman, M.B. (1995). Physiological origins and functional correlates of EEG rhythmic activities: Implications for self-regulation. *Applied Psychophysiology and Biofeedback* 21(1), 3–33.

Thompson, M. & Thompson, L. (2003). *The Neurofeedback Book: An introduction to basic concepts in applied psychophysiology*. Wheat Ridge, CO: Association for Applied Psychophysiology and Biofeedback.

Thompson, M. & Thompson, L. (2015). *The Neurofeedback Book: An introduction to basic concepts in applied psychophysiology*. Toronto: Association for Applied Psychophysiology and Biofeedback.

3

INTEGRATING NEUROCOUNSELING WITH ASSESSMENTS, TREATMENT PLANNING, AND OUTCOME EVALUATION

Theodore J. Chapin

Henry Ford, entrepreneur extraordinaire, once stated that "obstacles are those frightful things that you see when you take your eyes off the goal." These words are so true for the field of neurocounseling, and counseling, in general. It is paramount to the success of our profession that goal-setting be accomplished in a manner that can individualize and customize the treatment plan. Therefore, in order to select an appropriate neurocounseling intervention, counselors are encouraged to conduct a thorough assessment of the client's presenting problem. This is accomplished by administering a comprehensive psychosocial medical history, a neurological risk assessment, screening checklists, and, if available, baseline biofeedback measures of peripheral skin temperature and heart rate variability, as well as quantitative electroencephalographic (QEEG) assessment of current brainwave activity. While the psychosocial medical history, neurological risk assessment, and psychological checklists will provide sufficient understanding of a client's underlying neurological functioning and possible sources of neurological dysregulation, the addition of biofeedback and neurofeedback measures will provide a more accurate physiological indication of a client's dysregulation. With this information, an individually designed treatment plan can be developed and a targeted neurocounseling intervention more confidently selected. Once the neurocounseling intervention is completed, it can also guide the focus and breadth of outcome evaluation.

The following chapter will review in some detail the critical aspects of a comprehensive psychosocial medical history. It will present the Neurological Dysregulation Risk Assessment and illustrate its value in understanding the factors that lead to neurological dysregulation and the resulting symptoms experienced by clients. It will then briefly review several psychological and behavioral screening checklists and screening tools that allow the counselor to begin to prioritize the impact of neurological dysregulation on the client's behavior. Specific measures of physiological and neurological functioning will also be described to help focus case conceptualization and guide individualized treatment planning and selection of neurocounseling interventions. Finally, outcome evaluation will be discussed to help counselors and their clients track progress and assess improvement in neurological dysregulation toward resolution of their presenting problems.

Psychosocial Medical History

A comprehensive psychosocial medical history is important to begin to understand possible sources of neurological dysregulation that may underlie a client's presenting problems. An overview of a thorough psychosocial medical history was provided by Chapin and Russell-Chapin (2014) and Russell-Chapin (2017). Before conducting the history, a few simple client observations may provide useful insight into their overall neurological functioning. Are they anxious and over-activated or depressed and under-activated? What is the quality of their handshake? What is the temperature of their hand? What is the quality and pattern of their breathing? What is their posture and the tone and quality of their speech? If their handshake is soft, this may suggest a passive interpersonal orientation, depression, or an under-activated anterior cingulate. If their hand is cold, their breathing is shallow, their posture slouching forward and the tone and quality of their voice soft, this may suggest a sympathetically dominated peripheral nervous system with tendencies toward over-activation.

The psychosocial medical history begins with asking about problems with their mother's pregnancy with them, possible birth trauma, and any significant or chronic childhood illnesses. It asks about any history of hospitalization, surgery, and exposure to anesthesia. It explores past medication use, over-the-counter medication, food supplements, illegal substance use, alcohol consumption, and nicotine and caffeine use. It asks about time spent on I-technology, sleep patterns, diet, head injuries, and any history of seizure disorders or stroke. It explores current cognitive functioning, problems with short- and long-term memory, and loss of cognitive efficiency. It surveys family history of bipolar disorder, attention deficit hyperactivity disorder, depression, anxiety, and addiction. It reviews school history with special attention to developmental disorders, behavioral and learning problems, and areas of low achievement. It asks about more severe psychological problems including obsessive compulsive disorder, personality and borderline disorder, dissociative disorder, psychosis and schizophrenia, and bipolar disorder. Finally, it reviews any past episodes of suicidal and aggressive behavior, as well as past traumatic or emotionally overwhelming experiences.

While any one of these areas may be sufficient to cause significant neurological dysregulation and corresponding psychological, emotional, or behavioral problems, a few are especially critical. These include head injuries, emotional trauma, and lifestyle factors of substance use, I-technology, and sleep problems. Head injury, even experienced many years earlier, can cause persisting and multiple-source functional brainwave dysregulation, due to its coup-countercoup (site of trauma, opposite part of the brain, and temporal lobe impact) effect on the brain. Emotional trauma can result in either or both over-activation (anxiety and hypervigilance) and under-activation (inattention, avoidance, and depression). Prolonged medication use and substance abuse can also affect brainwave activation, requiring ongoing monitoring, special attention, or substance abuse treatment before neurocounseling intervention can become efficacious. Finally, excessive I-technology use (more than two hours a day beyond that required for school or work) and sleep problems (less than eight hours a night), left unaddressed, can also undermine effective neurocounseling intervention.

Other important considerations in assessment involve the influence of gender differences, quality of early parent-child interaction and later peer relationships, and unjust social systems characterized by poverty, increased exposure to neurotoxins, and long-term stress that are damaging to the neurological development of children and adult neurological functioning (Ivey, Bradford Ivey & Zalaquett, 2018). Women's brains appear to be three years younger than men's due to gender differences in glucose metabolism (Goyal et al., 2019) and men appear to have more gray matter or neuronal density, while women have more white matter or neuronal communication between different areas of the brain (Xin et al., 2019). This has implications for differences in cognition, emotional control, and related neurological disorders. Daniel Siegel, in his *Pocket Guide to Interpersonal Neurobiology: An Integrative Handbook of the Mind* (2012), presented overwhelming evidence stressing the vital importance of attachment and a reciprocal and responsive parent-child relationship in early healthy neurological development. He later extended this work to further explain how healthy interpersonal connections throughout adolescence, a critical period in brain remodeling, and adult life shape our neural connections and healthy brain functioning (Siegel, 2013). Poverty, with its increased exposure to neurotoxic chemicals, such as polycyclic aromatic hydrocarbons, and long-term stress due to child maltreatment, impoverished learning environments, and poor and inconsistent parenting due to multiple socio-economic factors, have also been found to cause adverse effects on brain development, maturation, and later adult functioning (Julvez et al., 2016). While more difficult to quantify, these aspects of a client's psychosocial medical history are also relevant in appreciation of the factors that impact their neurological dysregulation.

Neurological Dysregulation Risk Assessment

The Neurological Dysregulation Risk Assessment (NDRA) is a paper-and-pencil checklist designed to help clients identify possible sources of neurological dysregulation. It was first published by Chapin & Russell-Chapin in 2014 and has been updated for this publication (see Chapter 2). The 15 factors of the NDRA include genetic predispositions, pre-natal exposure, birth complications, disease and high fever, current diagnoses, poor diet, lack of exercise or sleep, emotionally suppressive psychosocial environment, head injury, prolonged life distress, stress-related disease, prolonged medication use, substance use or other addictions, seizures disorders, chronic pain, surgical anesthesia, chemotherapy and/or aging, and excessive I-technology and/or screen time. Each NDRA item describes in more detail examples of problems reflective of the factor.

Clients are instructed to read each potential source of neurological dysregulation and indicate whether or not it may be a risk factor in their life. Adults may also complete the checklist for their partner or child. The NDRA is scored by calculating the total number of "Yes" responses. The greater the number of "Yes" responses, the greater the likely risk of significant neurological dysregulation. However, clients are cautioned that even one "Yes" response may be sufficient to cause significant dysregulation and indicate the neurological basis of their current emotional, physiological, cognitive, or behavioral problems.

Consistent reports between the psychosocial medical history and the NDRA are noteworthy and warrant further review. Once confirmed and more fully explored, both the history and the NDRA results may lead to a preliminary identification of possible goals for neurocounseling intervention.

Screening Checklists

Several basic screening checklists may be useful in determining the relative presence of the psychological and behavioral consequences of neurological dysregulation. The most common checklists to employ provide an overall measure of anxiety, depression, trauma, attention, and symptoms. Other relevant measures may also be indicated, based upon the client's presenting issues, and made evident by the results of their psychosocial medical history and Neurological Dysregulation Risk Assessment (NDRA). Some of these include measures of insomnia, body perception, anger, executive function, and cognitive functioning, with the last three often important when there is suspicion of a head injury.

Anxiety

A simple, easily administered and scored, measure of anxiety is the Burns Anxiety Inventory (Burns, 1993). It consists of 33 items and takes about 15 minutes to complete. The instructions ask the client to rate each statement according to how much they have been bothered by that feeling in the last few days. The checklist surveys many physiological manifestations of anxiety such as a racing heart, sweaty palms, and detachment from one's bodily sensations. Clients report the degree to which they have experienced that feeling on a four-point scale of "not at all," "somewhat," "moderately," or "a lot." Total scores are calculated and indicate "absent to low, mild, moderate or severe" levels of anxiety.

Depression

A commonly used measure of depression is the Beck Depression Inventory, Second Edition (Beck, Steer & Brown, 1996). It also takes about 15 minutes to complete and consists of 21 items with four response options. Clients are asked to circle the response that best describes their current thoughts and feelings. Their total scores are calculated and indicate the severity of depressive symptoms from none to low, mild, moderate, or severe.

Trauma

Many trauma inventories are available for both children and adults. Some are self-report and others rely on parents' reports of their observations of their child's behavior. One measure for adults is the PCL Checklist (Weathers et al., 2013). It consists of 17 items and also takes about 15 minutes to complete. Clients are asked to review a list of problems and complaints people sometimes experience in response to a stressful life event. An example of one statement is, "Feeling jumpy or easily startled." They then rate, on a five-point scale, from "not at all," "a little bit," "moderately," "quite a bit," to "extremely," how much they have been bothered by that problem or complaint. A total score is then calculated and indicates the severity of symptoms associated with post-traumatic stress disorder from none to low, mild, moderate, or severe.

Attention

A brain-based checklist of attentional problems is the Amen Brain System Checklist based on the work of Daniel Amen (2013, 2014). It consists of 101 items that can be completed by the client or a significant other (spouse, partner, or parent). Clients are asked to rate symptoms on a scale of "never," "rarely," "occasionally," "frequently," and "very frequently." All ratings of "frequently" or "very frequently" are scored in the direction of the corresponding brain-based subtype of attentional problems. The seven subtypes are (1) inattention and (2) hyperactivity-impulsivity or (3) combined inattention and hyperactivity located in the prefrontal cortex, (4) obsessive compulsive located in the anterior cingulate, (5) depression in the deep limbic area, (6) anxiety in the basal ganglia, and (7) irritability and sensory problems in the temporal lobes.

Problem Checklist

The value of a problem checklist is that it can readily assess and compare the relative presence of many problems with one test. The neurologically based Problem Checklist and Symptom Rating Form (see Fig 2.2 in Chapter 2) is adapted from Paul Swingle's (2008) five-channel, Quick Q, later renamed, the Clinical Q (quantitative electroencephalogram). It consists of 62 problem statements, correlated to five major brain locations, which reflect over 95% of the problems clients present for treatment. These areas include the prefrontal cortex (F3, F4), the anterior cingulate (FZ), the sensory motor strip (CZ), and the occipital lobe (O1). Clients are asked to check all the problems they are experiencing, circle the top ten, and place a star by the top five. This helps the counselor both understand and prioritize the significance of a client's emotional, cognitive, and behavioral problems.

Other Potentially Relevant Measures

Insomnia

Many clients experience sleep problems. They either have insufficient sleep (less than eight hours a night), problems with sleep onset, shallow or poor sleep quality, and/or problems waking up. If sleep is identified as a problem, a sleep checklist may be helpful to assess the quality of their sleep. The Insomnia Severity Index (Morin et al., 2011) is a seven-item checklist that takes about five minutes to complete. Clients are asked to rate the severity of their sleep disruption in the last two weeks. This includes problems with falling asleep, nighttime awakening, and early morning arousal.

Body Perception

The Body Perception Questionnaire (Porges, 1993) is a measure of interoception or body awareness. It is also a method to understand a client's stress response, autonomic nervous system reactivity, stress style, and resulting health history. Clients who may be experiencing a fight, flight, or freeze reaction rate their perception of their body and its physiological responses. This provides the counselor with a thorough review of the client's physiological self-awareness and level of sympathetic activation.

Anger

The Anger Disorder Scale-Short (DiGiuseppe & Tafrate, 2004) is an 18-item screening tool of possible anger problems. Its value in neurocounseling assessment is that clients with a history of head injury often experience problems with anger. To complete the checklist, clients are asked to respond in a manner that "best describes them," by reporting the frequency with which they are experiencing typical symptoms of anger. Three measures of anger are generated. These include reactivity and expression, anger (held) in, vengeance, and a total anger score.

Executive Function

Also implicated in clients with head injury are problems with executive function. The Barkley Deficits in Executive Function Scale (Barkley, 2011) measures the impact of head injury on daily functioning for both adults and children. The test takes 15–20 minutes to complete. Clients rate the frequency with which they experience 89 different problems associated with executive function from "never or rarely," "sometimes," "often," to "very often." The test yields seven different measures of executive function. These include self-management to time, self-organization and problem solving, self-restraint, self-motivation, self-regulation of emotions, a total executive function score, and an ADHD-executive function index score.

Cognitive Functioning

A third factor in clients with head injury is its potential impact on cognitive functioning. The Cognistat (2015) allows rapid assessment of neurocognitive functioning. It can be administered in 15–30 minutes and provides information on orientation, attention, memory, and five ability areas: language (comprehension, repetition, and naming), constructional ability (drawing from memory and arranging tiles), memory, calculation skills, and executive skills (reasoning and judgment). The test can determine if clients are functioning in the average range or with mild, moderate, or severe impairment.

Baseline Measures of Physiological and Neurological Functioning

While the results of self-report, screening checklists, and paper-and-pencil testing of psychological and behavioral problems are sufficient and very helpful in guiding case conceptualization and treatment planning, baseline measures of physiological and neurological functioning offer a deeper and enhanced, behaviorally valid, assessment of a client's current functioning. This type of assessment typically requires more advanced training and experience with computer software and technology, biofeedback equipment, and quantitative electroencephalography. Counselors without this training and equipment should respect the limits of their competency and reach out and consult with appropriately qualified colleagues who can provide this assessment for their clients. Useful baseline measures of physiological and neurological functioning include a test of continuous performance, cognitive assessment, peripheral skin temperature, and heart rate variability assessment, and a quantitative electroencephalogram with LORETA imaging capability.

Test of Continuous Performance

One test of continuous performance is called the Test of Variable Attention or TOVA (Greenburg & Waldman, 1993). It is a computerized test of variable attention that compares a client's visual and auditory attentional functioning to a normative sample. It is often used in conjunction with other testing and clinical information to help diagnose attention deficit hyperactivity disorder. Since many physiological and neurological problems result in attentional deficits, it is also a good test to evaluate the overall impact of neurological dysregulation on visual and cognitive processing. The TOVA is administered in two parts, visual and auditory, and takes about 40 minutes to complete. Clients are asked to respond to each visual image by clicking a mouse, except when a certain image appears. The images are presented in a relatively slow and then quickened manner over four segments. Clients are also asked to respond to an auditory tone by clicking a mouse, except when a certain tone is heard. These sounds are also presented in a relatively slow and then quickened manner over four segments. When completed, the TOVA is automatically scored and reports, among other factors, errors in client omissions and commissions. That is, the number of times the client failed to respond when they should have or when they responded when they should not have. These scores can then be interpreted to determine if a client has a visual or auditory attentional problem and whether that problem is associated with general nervous system slowing or over-activation.

Cognitive Assessment

The Cambridge Brain Sciences (CBS, 2020) test of cognitive abilities is a brain-based, online tool that can be completed in 15 minutes. It assesses 12 core cognitive abilities organized in four key areas including memory (visuospatial working memory, spatial short-term memory, working memory, episodic memory), reasoning (mental rotation, visuospatial processing, deductive reasoning, planning), verbal ability (verbal reasoning, verbal short-term memory), and concentration (attention and response inhibition). Clients respond to engaging online tasks. The results are automatically scored, forwarded to the health care professional, and interpreted as below average, average, or above average. Clients can repeat the test over the length of their neurocounseling intervention and track meaningful changes in their cognitive ability that occur as a results of their treatment.

Peripheral Skin Temperature

Many methods of peripheral skin temperature assessment are available to counselors. These range from a small hand-held thermometer, to an inexpensive digital thermometer with a skin temperature sensor, up to expensive biofeedback equipment (Chapin and Russell-Chapin, 2014). Even an initial handshake with a client can offer a general reading of a client's peripheral skin temperature. When clients are stressed or in a sympathetic response pattern, their hand will feel cold and their peripheral skin temperature will likely be 84 degrees or lower. When clients are mildly calm their hand will feel neither particularly cold or warm. When they are relaxed or in a parasympathetic response pattern, their hand will feel warm and their peripheral skin temperature will likely be 90 degrees or higher. This is a useful way to determine a client's current level of physiological and neurological activation. An inexpensive digital thermometer with a skin sensor can be found at www.toolsforwellness.com/product/stressthermometer-temperature-biofeedback-digital-numeric-thermal-trainer/.

Heart Rate Variability

Heart rate variability (HRV) is a measure of the variation in time between heartbeats that reflects the amount of stress a client is experiencing (McCraty et al., 2009). A lower HRV, less time between beats, signifies a predominant activation of the sympathetic nervous system. A higher HRV, more time between beats, reflects a predominant activation of the parasympathetic (calm recovery) system. HRV also corresponds to breathing rates. The average adult breathing rate is between 12 and 20 breaths per minute. Abnormal adult breathing rates are above 20 breaths per minute and reflect sympathetic dominance. When adults are calmly relaxed their breathing rate can decrease to six and even four breaths per minute. Like peripheral skin temperature, a counselor can quickly assess a client's likely heart rate variability by simply observing their breathing pattern. This can be done by watching how their shoulder rises and falls or noticing if they breathe more from their chest or abdomen (referred to as diaphragmatic breathing). Clients who are over-activated often breathe from their chest and take many, short breaths. Clients who are calm and relaxed breathe more from their abdomen and take few, deeper breaths. HRV can be measured with more precision. The emWave, produced by the Institute of HeartMath (Boulder Creek, CA) is one example. It utilizes proprietary software and hardware, including a plethysmograph that measures blood flow from a fingertip or ear lobe sensor, and converts it into a breathing trace line that can be observed and quantified. Breathing, HRV, and autonomic functioning are interrelated systems. The term coherence has been used to characterize the bottom-up (body to brain) and top-down (brain to body) entrainment of diaphragmatic breathing, heart rate variability, and autonomic activation (McCraty et al., 2009). Assessing a client's positive (parasympathetic) or negative (sympathetic) coherence pattern is useful in establishing their goals for neurocounseling.

Quantitative Electroencephalography

A quantitative electroencephalogram (QEEG) is a method of assessing the brain's electrical activity related to a client's emotional, cognitive, psychological, and behavioral problems (Chapin & Russell-Chapin, 2014). Overall, the brain generates enough electrical activity to power a low wattage light bulb. A QEEG records the small amounts of electrical activity produced when neurons fire in specific locations and across neuronal networks, necessary for the performance of basic life functions. It then breaks down these brainwaves into specific frequencies and compares them to those of a clinical or general population. This allows the evaluator to draw conclusions about possible sources of neurological dysregulation related to a client's presenting problems.

The most common brainwave frequencies are delta, theta, alpha, sensory motor rhythm (SMR), low beta, high beta, and gamma waves. Delta waves occur between 0 and 3 Hz (cycles per minute). These slow waves are associated with sleep and neuronal sprouting. Theta waves occur between 4 and 7 Hz and are associated with inner states such as drowsiness and meditation. Alpha waves occur between 8 and 10 Hz and are associated with calm focus and cognitive efficiency. Alpha waves are also described as the idling brainwave and assist in the transition from inner to outer states of attention. Sensory motor rhythm (SMR) waves occur between 13 and 15 Hz and are associated with physical and perceptual calming. Persons with ADHD often have dysregulated SMR waves. Low beta waves occur between 15 and 20 Hz and are associated with healthy activation and problem solving. High beta waves occur from 20 Hz and above and are associated with anxiety, perseveration, and over-activation.

Gamma waves occur at about 40 Hz and are associated with insight, satisfaction from learning, pleasure, and happiness.

In general, healthy neurological regulation involves engaging the right brainwave, at the right time, for the right task. Neurological dysregulation involves being stuck in the wrong brainwave, at the wrong time, for the wrong task. For example, to fall asleep, a healthily regulated person will calm their body and mind, generate more theta waves to create drowsiness, and then slide into delta wave states for deep recovering sleep. An unhealthy, dysregulated person, when trying to fall asleep, may get stuck in excessive beta wave or "busy brain" activity, being unable to calm their physical body and thoughts. They cannot readily generate inner states of drowsiness, and this prevents them from falling and staying asleep. Specialized training and experience is required to conduct a QEEG assessment, but the information it generates can both identify problem brain locations and specify the brainwave interventions necessary to help correct the dysregulation.

A five-channel, or five-location, Clinical QEEG is clinically normed, and can provide sufficient treatment plan information for 95% of the clients who present for neurocounseling (Swingle, 2008). It takes about 20 minutes to administer and generates a narrative report on five key brain locations. These include the frontal lobes (F3, F4), the anterior cingulate (FZ), the sensory motor strip (CZ), and the occipital lobe (O1). The clinical normative base compares the client's results to persons with known clinical problems, thus increasing the likely validity of five-channel QEEG results.

The 19-channel, or 19-location, QEEG is normed on the general population. It is most helpful when more global brain dysregulation is suspected. Some examples of presenting problems that may reflect more global dysregulation are head injury, oxygen deprivation, high fever, and substance abuse. It takes about an hour to administer and generates a color-coded visual representation or brain map of likely neurological dysregulation. The same general procedures are employed to collect the EEG data, but a cap with 19 different sensors is placed on the client's head and the results must be interpreted by a specially trained technician. The general population norm compares the client's results to the general population. One popular normative data base is Neuroguide, developed by Bob Thatcher et al. (1989, 2003). If the client's score falls one and a half to two standard deviations from the norm, it suggests that their result likely indicates a significant source of neurological dysregulation.

An additional application of quantitative electroencephalography is the functional brain imaging technique called LORETA or low-resolution electromagnetic tomography. LORETA was originally described by Pascual-Marqui, Michel & Lehman (1994). It uses the surface electrode data collected from the 19-channel QEEG to determine the relative electrical activity of deeper regions of the brain. With this information, LORETA can generate a real-time, three-dimensional model of a client's cortical activity. This is especially important because it allows the counselor and client to see, in real time, a three-dimensional visual image of the client's brain both before and after a neurocounseling intervention.

Treatment Planning

There are four steps in comprehensive neurocounseling treatment planning: prioritizing the presenting problems, determining the brain locations that are implicated from the assessment of neurological dysregulation, selecting a neurocounseling intervention, and identifying behavioral goals for coaching clients on ways to improve their neuroplasticity. While neurocounseling interventions may improve a client's underlying neurological dysregulation, they are not a substitute for the effectiveness of conventional counseling interventions to provide the skills and supportive interpersonal environment for clients to fully achieve the life changes they seek. In many cases, clients who have struggled with making these changes through counseling alone will often find that strengthened neurological regulation will help them more successfully apply the lessons of therapy in their lives.

Prioritizing Presenting Problems

Prioritization of a client's presenting problems begins with review and summarization of the neurocounseling assessment results. The psychosocial medical history will help the counselor initially identify possible sources of neurological dysregulation. The client responses that provide an affirmative indication can be first listed on a Client Treatment Plan Summary (see Fig 3.1). Next, the results of the Neurological

Dysregulation Risk Assessment can be reviewed with its affirmative responses also listed in the Client Treatment Plan. Note that some of these items may repeat, suggesting some concurrent validation of the client's self-report. The results of the screening checklists are now considered and added to the Treatment Plan Summary. These add another level of concurrent validation but, more importantly, begin to help objectively quantify and prioritize the relative presence of the presenting problems. Special attention and notation should be made to the significant results and the client's own prioritization of their presenting problems from the Problem Checklist, with these highlighted in the Treatment Plan Summary. It is very common for the client's prioritization of their own problems to be consistent with the results of the Screening Checklist. On some occasions, an obvious mismatch may be observed. This may be related to a client's denial or lack of psychological insight into their own experiences.

An even deeper level of concurrent validation involves review and notation of any significant results found in the Baseline of Physiological and Neurological Functioning and the results of the Quantitative Electro-encephalography, if available for inclusion in the treatment plan. These provide a current assessment of the physiological impact of the client's neurological dysregulation and a direct assessment of the location and nature of that dysregulation. Although very helpful for a focused and strongly valid treatment plan, should these assessment resources be unavailable to the counselor, the aforementioned assessment may be sufficient in the identification of likely brain locations from the Head Map of Functions.

Head Map of Functions

The Head Map of Functions in Figure 3.2 illustrates the various brain locations, as defined by the International 10–20 System (Jasper, 1958) and their functions as defined by John Anderson (2018). Please note that the Head Map of Functions is presented on an outline of a human head with the nose or nasion at due north, the inion or back of the head at due south, and the ears at due west and east. The Head Map of Functions is also organized by a system of coordinates. Each coordinate has a letter (or letters) and a number, forming a grid across the brain. The

Client Treatment Plan Summary

Client Name: _____   Age: _____   DOB: _____
Counselor Name: _____   Date: _____

Psychosocial Medical History (Top 10 Indicated Items)

1. _____   6. _____
2. _____   7. _____
3. _____   8. _____
4. _____   9. _____
5. _____   10. _____

Neurological Dysregulation Risk Assessment (Top 6 Indicated Items)

1. _____   4. _____
2. _____   5. _____
3. _____   6. _____

Basic Screening Checklists (circle)

Anxiety:	__Average	__Moderate	__Severe
Depression:	__Average	__Moderate	__Severe
Trauma:	__Average	__Moderate	__Severe
Attention:	__Average	__Moderate	__Severe

Problem Checklist and Symptom Rating Form
Top Three Symptoms: _____ _____ _____
Other Top Seven Symptoms: _____ _____ _____
_____ _____ _____ _____

Other Relevant Measures (conclusion)
Insomnia: _____
Body Perception: _____
Anger: _____
Executive Function: _____
Cognitive Functioning: _____

Baseline Measurement of Physiological and Neurological Functioning
Test of Continuous Performance: Visual____ (over/under-activated) Auditory____ (over/under-activated)
CBS Cognitive Assessment (Below average scores): __
Peripheral Skin Temperature: Degree/Rating   __84< = Tense   __Average   __90> = Relaxed
Heart Rate Variability: __Sympathetic Response __Parasympathetic Response
5 Channel QEEG (Problem Areas) :   __ F3   __F4   __FZ   __ CZ   __O1
19 Channel QEEG (Additional Problem Areas): _____

Prioritization of Presenting Problems (Top 3)
1. _____ 2. _____ 3. _____

Identification of Head Map of Functions (Locations and Functions)
1. _____ 2. _____ 3. _____

Selection of Neurocounseling Interventions
1. _____ 2. _____ 3. _____

Coaching of Behavioral Changes to Increase Neuroplasticity

___ Food Supplements	___Diet	__Relaxation/Meditations Strategies
___Sleep	___Substance Use	__Social Interactions
___Exercise	___Screen Time	__Intellectual Challenge

Figure 3.1 Client Treatment Plan Summary

letters of the coordinates represent the various areas of the brain, where F stands for the frontal lobes with FP representing the prefrontal cortex, C stands for the sensory motor strip, T for the temporal lobes, P for the parietal lobes, and O for the occipital lobes. The numbers are organized with even numbers assigned to the right hemisphere and odd numbers assigned to the left hemisphere. An understanding of this coordinate grid system is important to make sense of the location of the neurocounseling interventions described in this book.

It is further important to note that while the Head Map of Functions is a two-dimensional representation of brain function locations, the LORETA images presented in this book are three dimensional. LORETA thus extends counselors' conceptual understanding of brain functioning from a topological viewpoint, to a depth or spatially, three-dimensionally illustrated perspective. This also serves to remind counselors that the brain functions with both gray matter, or specialized locational function, and white matter, or network communication function across the brain.

Counselors are strongly encouraged to familiarize themselves with the International 10–20 System coordinate grid and the functional descriptions of each brain location. It is only with an in-depth understanding of the functional descriptions of the Head Map of Functions, that counselors will be able to translate the assessment results into their corresponding brain locations and targeted neurocounseling interventions.

Selecting Neurocounseling Interventions

The selection of neurocounseling interventions follows directly from the assessment results and their corresponding relevance to the Head Map of Functions. With consideration of the client's prioritized problems from the Problem Checklist, the results of the Neurological Dysregulation Assessment, the relative presence of significant problems from the Behavioral Checklists, the Baseline Physiological and Neurological Functioning, and the Quantitative Electroencephalography results (if available), the counselor reviews the Head Map of Functions location descriptions and selects the primary locations for neurocounseling intervention.

In general, anxiety problems will likely be best addressed in the right frontal and right hemisphere locations; depression will be best addressed

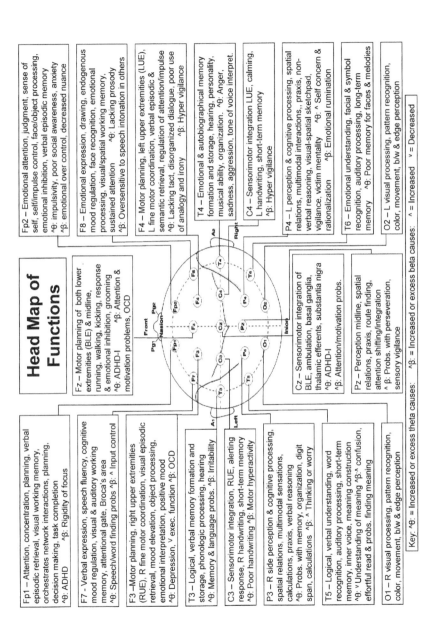

Figure 3.2 Head Map of Functions

in the left frontal and left hemisphere locations; obsessive compulsive problems are addressed at the front and midline locations; sleep problems are addressed at both the sensory motor strip and the occipital lobe; emotional trauma along the midline and at the occipital lobe; and attentional or problems with cognitive efficiency can be best addressed at the frontal lobes or sensory motor strip.

A client's initial and ongoing response to a specific neurocounseling intervention will also guide the counselor with valuable feedback in implementing the treatment plan. In some cases, meaningful change may be observed very quickly or an aversive reaction may become quickly evident. Despite the breadth or validity of the assessment results, a client's reactions to the selected intervention is the best barometer for verification of an effective location and intervention.

Coaching on Behavioral Changes to Increase Neuroplasticity

The psychosocial medical history and the Neurological Dysregulation Risk Assessment can provide useful information in understanding a client's baseline neuroplasticity. Lower baseline neuroplasticity will likely inhibit progress from the neurocounseling interventions and increased neuroplasticity will facilitate it. Children with less exposure to life's dysregulating influences often present with better neuroplasticity than adults, who have frequently experienced many of life's dysregulating effects. Some of the primary issues for coaching toward improved neuroplasticity include dietary supplements, sleep, exercise, diet, substance use, screen time, relaxation or medication strategies, social interaction, and intellectual challenge.

Many authors have summarized numerous strategies for optimal neurological functioning and neuroplasticity. Rock et al. (2012) described their model as "The Healthy Mind Platter for Optimal Brain Matter." Chapin & Russell-Chapin (2014) wrote of "Strategies for Self-regulation." Ivey, Ivey & Zalaquett (2018) described 17 "Therapeutic Lifestyle Changes," and Russell-Chapin (2017) wrote about "Wellness and Optimal Performance." These resources provide much of the basic research documenting the behavioral changes that can improve neuroplasticity.

Some of the most important food supplements for improving neuroplasticity include omega 3 fatty acids, curcumin or turmeric, or vitamin D, N-acetylcysteine (NAC), and melatonin. Omega 3s and curcumin have anti-inflammatory properties that support improved neurological and immunological functioning. Vitamin D has been found to also improve immunological functioning and assist in the regulation of circadian cycles. NAC directly supports neurological functioning and aids in glutamatergic functioning of neurons. Melatonin is a hormone that assists in the wake-sleep cycle and is often suggested for persons with sleep problems, promoting access to deeper recovery stages of sleep. Some caution should be exercised in suggesting food supplements. It may be best to have clients consult a physician or homeopathic specialist to avoid any unforeseen interaction with prescribed medications.

Sleep is critically important for physiological recovery, immunological functioning, memory consolidation, and cognitive efficiency. Seven to eight hours is recommended for adults, nine to eleven for school-aged children, and eight to ten for teens. If sleep is a problem for a client, it is best that that problem be addressed first because good, healthy sleep provides the foundation for all other change.

A minimum of 20 minutes of daily aerobic exercise is recommended for everyone. Exercise has been found to have strong physical, neuro-logical, cognitive, and mental health benefits. Forty minutes of aerobic exercise, three times a week stimulates the brain's production of Brain Derived Neurotropic Factor (BDNF), "Miracle Gro" for neurogenesis (Ratey, 2008). Daily exercise, especially with a partner, has been found to be as effective as antidepressant medication for the treatment of chronic depression.

Excessive consumption of simple carbohydrates and sugar has been found to have adverse effects on neurological functioning, memory, and neuroplasticity. The healthiest diet for optimal brain functioning relies on lean protein, complex carbohydrates (vegetables and berries), and saturated-monounsaturated fats (coconut and olive oil).

Alcohol, nicotine, caffeine, illegal drugs, and long-term medication use can cause neurological dysregulation. Over time, these can effect both the function and structure of the brain. While some research has indicated that moderate consumption of alcohol – one drink a day for women and two for men – may have some health benefits, some clients may become dependent on alcohol or other substances to help regulate emotional and physiological stress. In the same way, many medications, while intending to treat a medical or psychological condition, may in time undermine the brain's ability to self-regulate its own physiological and neurological functioning. In addition, although now legal in many states, marijuana use is particularly harmful to the developing brains of teenagers and young adults. Even excessive use by older adults can result in the same neurological dysregulation as longer-term alcohol abuse. Clients with these issues may benefit from other non-substance approaches for emotional and physical self-regulation.

Excessive use of screens, two or more hours a day beyond what is needed for school or work, has been found to cause significant neurological dysregulation, loss of cognitive efficiency, and depression. Some research has found that excessive screen time, especially related to video-game playing, social media, and frequent scrolling behavior, can reduce key brainwave functioning and result in brainwave patterns similar to inattentive ADD, marijuana dependence, and early-onset dementia.

There are many relaxation and meditation strategies to improve both the function and structure of the brain. These include general muscle relaxation, guided mental imagery, meditation or prayer, peripheral skin temperature training, diaphragmatic breathing, heart rate variability training, therapeutic harmonics, audio-visual entrainment, transcranial direct current stimulation, and neurofeedback training. Many neurocounseling interventions employ these strategies.

Social and community interaction has been found by many researchers to be vitally important in healthy attachment, emotional, interpersonal, physical, and neurological functioning. Connecting time in "face to face" relationships, with life-long friends, in strong marriages, and with community organizations can improve blood pressure, cardiovascular, endocrine, and immune system functioning. It has also been found to increase longevity by up to nine years. In addition, the social engagement system (Porges, 2011) and counseling relationships (Ivey, Ivey & Zalaquett, 2018) have been found to facilitate calm-recovery states of parasympathetic functioning, a precursor for healthy interpersonal and neurological functioning. Unfortunately, its absence has also been found to be deleterious to socioeconomically and culturally disadvantaged populations.

Finally, intellectual challenge has also been found to promote neuroplasticity. Intellectual challenge involves cognitive activity that stimulates neuronal sprouting, activation, and growth. Lesser challenged neurons looks like a struggling tree with few roots, a slim trunk, and sparse branches. A more strongly challenged neuron looks like a tree with deep reaching and spreading roots, a wide healthy trunk, and expansive branches. Intellectual challenge involves more complex tasks such as learning a new language, taking up a musical instrument, and engaging novel environments.

Neurocounseling Outcome Evaluation

Outcome evaluation in neurocounseling can be complicated and challenging for a few reasons. Clients may not recognize that they have changed, but those around them often notice significant differences in their behavior, emotional regulation, interpersonal interaction, and/or cognitive functioning. While neurocounseling has been found to stimulate subtle changes in neurological functioning, these often occur below a client's level of awareness. Neurological change during the course of neurocounseling is incrementally progressive and does not typically generalize until well beyond the last neurocounseling session. This occurs because after the last session, the client has only just begun to use their more effectively functioning brain in their daily life. Over time, environmental feedback inevitably reinforces both a client's neurological and behavioral change, bringing to conscious awareness what was previously imperceptible, allowing its generative benefits to become more obvious. It is also important to appreciate that even subtle neurological change can result in significant behavioral change because neurological change and behavioral change are not necessarily linear. Even a small amount of neurological change may be sufficient to break through a previously stagnant behavioral threshold. The inverse is also true. Sometimes large amounts of neurological change are insufficient to cause a marked behavioral change. Therefore several types of outcome evaluation are best employed to assess both objective neurological, physiological, emotional, and behavioral change, and a client's subjective experience of change.

Objective Assessment of Change

Objective assessment of change can occur at many levels. The basic level involves re-administration or post-testing of the primary screening checklists including the Burns's Anxiety Inventory, the Beck Depression Inventory, the PCL Trauma Checklist, and the Amen Brain System Checklist. While these rely on the client's self-report, they are normed and therefore provide some valid appraisal of pre- to post-neurocounseling intervention. Given the previously noted possibility that a client may not perceive much change immediately following the last counseling session, it may be best to hold off post-testing until several weeks after the final session, or conduct the post-testing both immediately following the last session and several weeks later. The same rationale can be applied to post-testing with other relevant measures involving insomnia, body perception, anger, executive function, and cognitive functioning.

A deeper level of objective post-test assessment involves re-administration of the baseline measurements of physiological and neurological functioning. Since these do not rely on a client's self-report, they offer a more valid evaluation of post-intervention change. These measures include the computerized test of variable attention, the more thorough CBS assessment of cognitive ability, peripheral skin temperature and heart rate variability assessment, and the five- and 19-channel (location) quantitative EEG. As previously noted, many counselors do not have the resources, ready access, or training to administer these measures. In such situations, counselors may refer their clients to other duly trained professionals for this assessment. Also note that post-testing of this nature takes time and is very expensive. While clients may readily offer their time and pay for the initial evaluation to develop their individualized treatment plan, they may not feel the value of such post-testing is worth the time or expense. Finally, as with the screening checklists, it may be worthwhile to consider either delaying post-testing until several weeks after the last neurocounseling session, or if resources allow, conduct it both immediately following the last session and several weeks later.

Client Self-Report of Change

As noted above, there is demonstrable reason to include assessment of a client's self-report of change. The most efficient way of doing so is by repeating the administration of the Problem Checklist and Symptom Rating Form as a post-test, immediately following the last session and several weeks later. It may also be helpful to administer the Problem

Checklist and Symptom Rating Form every ten sessions during active neurocounseling intervention. This allows both the counselor and the client to track progress over time and alert them to any setbacks that may become evident through the checklist results. Given the subtle and non-linear relationship between neurological and behavioral change, there is a strong argument to be made that the client's self-report of change is the most valuable, timely, and economic source of outcome information available to both.

Observational Information

A final source of outcome assessment is counselor observation and third-party reports of client change. Although this is not objectively valid information, it is often a very moving source of feedback to both the counselor and client. During neurocounseling work clients may offer very compelling observations and comments about their life. They may report improved sleep and increased dreaming, a sign of improved neurological regulation. They may report fewer conflicts at home or periods of unexpected happiness. They may talk about breakthroughs in their personal relationships, coming to important life decisions, or simply report unexpected behavior like cleaning the silverware, organizing their closets, or enjoying a good book which they had previously set aside. Other observations and comments by third parties are also sometimes very telling. These may include a teacher's report that a child has been much calmer and comfortable participating in a class, a psychiatrist who expresses surprise at a client's remarkable progress following neurocounseling, a spouse who relays more satisfaction in quiet conversation with their partner, or a doctor who requests the counselor's confirmation that a reduction in medication appears warranted. In some ways these kinds of third-party observations and comments are more validating to client and counselors than other objective and self-report checklist results.

Conclusions

Assessment, treatment planning, and outcome evaluation are very important in the process of neurocounseling. They guide the counselor in understanding the nature of the client's presenting concern and underlying neurological dysregulation. They illustrate and widen the counselor's conceptualization of both the encephalographic topological and three-dimensional LORETA view of brain function. They help direct the counselor's attention to specific brain locations, their neurological function, and the neurocounseling interventions which may help re-regulate the client's physiological, behavioral, emotional, interpersonal, and cognitive functioning. While significant change is the ultimate goal of neurocounseling, the process of assessment can take many meaningful forms. These may include objective assessment, subjective self-report, and third-party observation. The timing of meaningful change can also be elusive. It may occur during neurocounseling, immediately following it, or many weeks later, after the client has had the opportunity to experience environmental feedback from the benefits of neurological re-regulation in their life.

Sometimes, neurocounseling may not be sufficient to help clients reach their goals. They may arrive with weak levels of neuroplasticity, due to aversive lifestyle influences and experiences. They may first need coaching to help change these behaviors and strengthen their core neuroplasticity. They may need more extensive clinical neurofeedback to help restore foundational neurological dysregulation. They may also need conventional counseling, either before or after neurocounseling, to reduce immobilizing psychosocial distress, learn new coping strategies, or to experience the trust of a supportive professional relationship that can help guide them through the sometimes overwhelming process of personal change.

References

Amen, D. (2013). *Healing ADD: The breakthrough program that allows you to see and help the seven types of ADD* (revised edition). New York: Penguin Group (USA).

Amen, D. (2014). *Amen Brain System Checklist*. Retrieved April 14, 2020 from www.drsusanmarra.com/wp-content/uploads/2014/10/Amen Brain.pdf.

Anderson, J. (2018). *Head Map of Functions*. Personal communication.

Barkley, R.A. (2011). *Barkley Deficiencies in Executive Function Scale (BDEFS-LF)*. New York: Guilford Press.

Beck, A.T., Steer, R.A. & Brown, G.K. (1996). *Manual for the Beck Depression Inventory-II*. San Antonio, TX: Psychological Corporation.

Burns, D.D. (1993). *Ten Days to Self-Esteem*. New York: Quill.

CBS (2020). Cambridge Brain Sciences (CBS). Toronto. Retrieved from www.cambridgebrainsciences.com.

Chapin, T.J. & Russell-Chapin, L. (2014). *Neurotherapy and Neurofeedback: Brain-based treatment for psychological and behavioral problems*. New York: Routledge.

Cognistat (2015). *2015 Cognistat Manual*. Montreal: Cognistat Inc.

DiGiuseppe, R. & Tafrate, R.C. (2004). *Anger Disorders Scale (ADS): Technical manual*. North Tonawand, NY: Multihealth Systems.

Goyal, M.S., Blazey, T.M., Su, Y., Couture, L.E., Durbin, T.J., Batemen, R.J., Benzinger, T.L.S., Morris, J.C., Raichle, M.E. & Vlassenko, A.G. (2019). Persistent metabolic youth in the aging female brain. *Proceedings of the National Academy of Sciences*. DOI:10.1073/pnas, 1815917116.

Greenburg, L.M. & Waldman, I.D. (1993). Developmental normative data on the Test of Variable Attention (TOVA). *Journal of Child Psychology and Psychiatry* 34, 1019–1030.

Ivey, A.E., Ivey Bradford, M. & Zalaquett, C. (2018). *Intentional Interviewing and Counseling* (9th ed). Boston, MA: Cengage Learning.

Jasper, H.H. (1958). Report of the committee on methods of clinical examination in electroencephalography. *Electroencephalography and Clinical Neurophysiology* 10(2), 370–375. DOI:10.1016.0013-4694(58)90053-1.

Julvez, J., Paus, T., Bellinger, D., Eskenazi, B., Tiemeier, H., Pearce, N., Ritz, B., White, T., Ramchandani, P., Domingo Gispert, J., Desrivieres, S., Brouwer, R., Boucher, O., Alamany, S., Lopez-Vicenta, M., Suades-Gonzales, E., Forns, J., Grandjuean, P. & Sunyer, J. (2016). Environment and brain development: Challenges in the global context. *Neuroepidemiology* 46, 79–82. DOI:10.1159/000442256.

McCraty, R., Atkinson, M., Tomasino, D. & Bradley, R.T. (2009). The coherent heart: Heart-brain interactions, psychophysiological coherence, and the emergence of system-wide order. *Integral Review* 5(2), 10–115.

Morin, C.M., Belleville, G., Belanger, L. & Ives, H. (2011). The Insomnia Severity Index: Psychometric indicators to detect insomnia cases and evaluate treatment response. *Sleep* 34, 601–608.

Pascual-Marque, R.D., Michel, C.M. & Lehmann, D. (1994). Low resolution electromagnetic tomography: A new method for localizing electrical activity in the brain. *International Journal of Psychophysiology* 18, 49–65.

Porges, S. (1993). Body perception questionnaire. Retrieved April 14, 2020 from www/stephenporges.com.

Porges, S. (2011). *The Polyvagal Theory*. New York: Norton.

Ratey, J.J. (2008). *Spark: The revolutionary new science of exercise and the brain*. New York: Little Brown.

Rock, D., Seigel, D.J., Poelman, S.A.Y. & Payne, J. (2012). The healthy mind platter. *Neuroleadership Journal* 4, 1–23.

Russell-Chapin, L. (2017). Neurocounseling assessment. In T.A. Field, L.K. Jones, and L. Russell-Chapin (eds.), *Neurocounseling: Brain-based clinical approaches*, pp. 115–131. Alexandria, VA: American Counseling Association.

Siegel, D.J. (2012). *Pocket Guide to Interpersonal Neurobiology: An integrative handbook of the mind*. New York: W.W. Norton.

Siegel, D.J. (2013). *Brainstorm: The power and purpose of the teenage brain*. New York: Jeremy P. Tarcher/Penguin, a member of Penguin Group (USA).

Swingle, P. (2008). *Basic Neurotherapy: The clinician's guide*. Vancouver, BC.

Thatcher, R.W., Walker, R.A., Biver, C.J., North, D.M. & Curtin, R. (2003). Sensitivity and specificity of the neuroguide EEG normative database: Validation and clinical correlation. *Journal of Neurotherapy* 7(3–4), 87–121.

Thatcher, R.W., Walker, R.A., Gerson, I. & Geisler, F. (1989). EEG discriminant analysis of mild head trauma. *Electroencephalography and Clinical Neurophysiology* 73, 93–106.

Weathers, F.W., Litz, B.T., Keane, T.M. Palmieri, P.A. Marx, B.P. & Schnurr, P.P. (2013). The PTSD checklist for DSM-5 (PCL-5), Retrieved April 14, 2020 from www.ptsd.va.gov/professional/assessment/adult-sr/ptsd-checklist.asp.

Xin, J., Zhang, Y., Tang, Y. & Yang, Y. (2019). Brain differences between man and women: Evidence from deep learning. *Frontiers of Neuroscience* 13(185). DOI:10.3389/fnins.2019,00185.

PART II

NEUROCOUNSELING APPLICATIONS

4

PREFRONTAL CORTEX (FP1 AND FP2)

Leading with the CEO of the Brain

Christine Nave and Jason DeFord

According to authors and clinicians Ted Chapin and Lori Russell-Chapin (2014) we need "to better understand the biological basis of behavior and learn how to harness its potential for our clients' benefit." That statement underlies the entire premise of this book. For our purpose here, the place to begin is the Prefrontal Cortex (FP1 and FP2). Understanding how these two sites and functions impact our daily lives is critical to healthy living, but it is also critical for helping professionals to better understand how to intentionally deliver counseling interventions. Both FP1 and FP2 will be analyzed.

FP1

The FP1 site is located at the very front left hemisphere of the brain (Figure 4.1). It is the core location of a person's personality; therefore, this location plays a crucial role in the success and failure of human endeavors. Significant responsibilities of the FP1 location are attention,

concentration, decision making, planning, task completion, verbal episodic retrieval, and visual working memory (Chapin & Chapin-Russell,
2014). An effective executive frontal cortex focuses on strengths where
one can overcome negative encounters through positive outcomes (Ivey
et al., 2009). Its primary activity is considered to be a choreography
of thoughts and actions in collaboration with internal goals. Humans
are unable to do similar things simultaneously due to a competition for
the same neurons, and the prefrontal cortex disengages attention from
one task and routes it to another task (Carter, 2019). Further, the frontal
cortex has the strongest projections to the amygdala, which forms a network called the "social brain."

Implications of Dysregulation

The brain is a sensitive, high-functioning organ that requires healthy nurturing throughout our lifespan. Without care and nurturing, dysregulation
can happen. Dysregulation occurs when there is an interruption in the

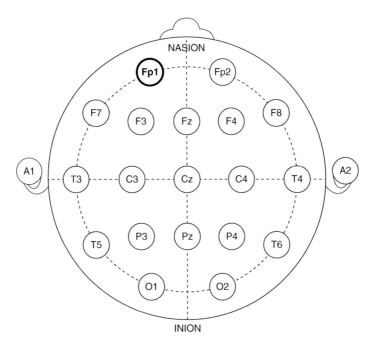

Figure 4.1 Head map graphic highlighting FP1 site

communication between neurons and brain structures, causing less firing of mirror neurons (Ivey et al., 2009). Chronic high-level or unpredictable stressors can disrupt self-regulatory systems due to ongoing exposure to stress hormones (Bridgett et al., 2015). Common mental health diagnoses associated with dysregulation in the frontal lobe/prefrontal cortex are the following: depression, ADHD, OCD, schizophrenia, bipolar disorder, traumatic brain injury, personality disorders, and PTSD. Clients may also have severe anxiety and paranoia as a result of an overactive amygdala connected with trauma and neglect. Clients present as if they are "in a fog," with difficulty in concentration, completing tasks, and become unmotivated and disconnected. Individuals high in impulsivity tend to react without thought or consideration of implications or consequences of their statements or behaviors. Damage to the frontal lobe can cause the following symptoms: speech problems, poor coordination, changes in personality, difficulties with impulse control, and trouble planning or sticking to a schedule (Villines, 2017). When dysregulation is noted in a person at FP1, rigidity of focus is often noted due to an increase, or excess, of beta waves. When trying to identify theta wave dysregulation, increased activity can lead to attention deficit hyperactivity disorder (ADHD).

Two Neurocounseling Interventions

Reframing

Reframing is an insightful way of reflecting on emotional events and thoughts while searching for positive outcomes and changes through self-awareness. Individuals high in impulsivity tend to react without thought or consideration of implications or consequences of their statements or behaviors (Bridgett et al., 2015). Regular practice of reframing takes time, effort, and self-discipline; however, it can promote self-regulation, improving mood and behavior (Bloom & Bloom, 2007).

Step 1: Ask your client to identify a negative past event in as much detail as possible and as objectively as possible. This is important as many negative events become much worse in our own minds due to cognitive distortions.

Step 2: Explore with your client how this past event could have been different. Challenge the cognitive distortions and explore how changing initial thoughts could cause the accompanying feelings and behaviors to have changed as well.

Step 3: Retell the new story that includes positive and healthy thoughts and decisions. Replay the event in the new light and process how this would have played out differently or been less debilitating for your client.

Step 4: Even though the event does not change, the perception, behavior, and decision making with future events have the potential for a positive outcome. Encourage your client to write out future events and work through the steps in order to challenge their negative perceptions.

Length of intervention: 30–50 minutes

Task Breakdown/Planner

Task breakdown, along with using a journal/planner, can be a useful tool in improving organization and planning. Problem solving is a positive clinical intervention that focuses on training in constructive skills with the goal to enhance psychological and behavioral functioning to prevent relapses and maximize quality of life (Nezu, Nezu & D'Zurilla, 2006). A small routine task can be overwhelming for the client with focus, planning, and organization challenges. Problem solving is an intervention which focuses on adaptive problem-solving skills (Bell & D'Zurilla, 2009) (Figure 4.2).

Step 1: Define a single task with your client. Be specific as to what the parameters are and why this needs to be accomplished. Avoid defining more than one task at a time.

Step 2: Break this task into smaller parts. As you work to break a larger task down, it becomes more manageable and less overwhelming. For example, cleaning the house sounds overwhelming, but breaking it down into washing dishes and doing laundry seems more feasible.

Step 3: Create a schedule. Connect each part of the task to a specific time or event (i.e., 4 P.M. or when I get home from work). In

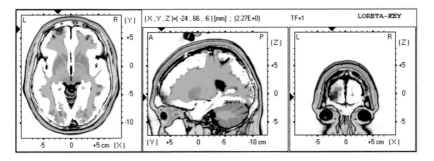

Figure 4.2 LORETA scans of FP1 during task breakdown intervention

addition, identify how your client will remember to do so, such as setting a phone reminder or writing out a post-it note.

Step 4: Prepare for the task. Identify how to eliminate distractions, plan for what-ifs, gather materials needed, and/or how to best prepare for the task.

Step 5: Imagine the outcome. Play out and try to experience the positive feelings and sense of accomplishment from completing both the individual parts and the bigger task.

Length of intervention: 30–50 minutes

FP2 Location and Function

The FP2 site is located in the right hemisphere of the frontal lobe, as part of the prefrontal cortex (Figure 4.3). The prefrontal cortex is the last part of the human brain to become fully active, and full myelinization, the sheathing of neuronal connections that allows information to flow freely along them, does not occur until a person is in their late twenties or early thirties (Carter, 2019). The frontal lobes interact with the amygdala as part of the social brain, as well as controlling our executive functions. As part of the larger frontal lobe system, the FP2 function will help with emotional attention, judgment, sense of self, self/impulse control, face/object processing, emotional inhibition, and verbal episodic memory (Chapin & Russell-Chapin, 2014). Once the prefrontal cortex has matured, healthy FP2 functioning will help in allowing a more thoughtful and deliberate response, whereas prior to maturity, a child might be overwhelmed by emotion.

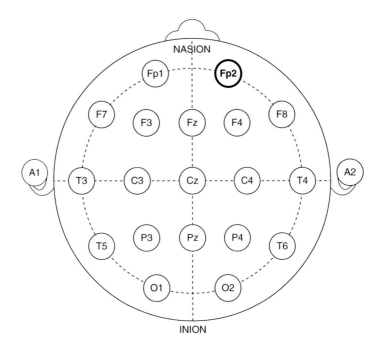

Figure 4.3 Head map graphic highlighting FP2 site

Implications of Dysregulation

In order to effectively help our clients, it is important to understand how the symptoms they are experiencing can be associated with a certain dysregulation in the brain. To get an accurate depiction of what the dysregulation is, a 19-channel EEG may be needed. This may not always be possible though, and therefore we can look at commonly identified symptoms and clinical implications of dysregulation at FP2 as related to what brainwave functions may be affected. Two brainwave bands that we think about in relation to dysregulation at FP2 are theta and beta. Theta waves are typically noted to be between 3 and 7 Hz (Swingle, 2008) and at the high end are related to reduced activity and involved in global thinking, spontaneity, daydreams, inattention, absence of directed thought, and meditation, while the lower end is related to depression, anxiety, and drowsiness (Chapin & Russell-Chapin, 2014). Beta waves are typically noted to be between 16 and 25 Hz (lobeta) and 28 and 40 Hz (hibeta) and related to information processing and problem solving

(Swingle, 2008), as well as focus, analysis, relaxed thinking, and external orientation (Demos, 2005). When dysregulation is noted in a person at FP2, anxiety is often noted due to an increase, or excess, of beta waves. In addition to anxiety, an increase of beta wave activity can also cause problems associated with emotional over-control and decreased nuance. When trying to identify theta wave dysregulation, increased activity can lead to impulsivity (ADHD symptoms) and poor social awareness.

Two Neurocounseling Interventions

As mentioned previously, anxiety is often seen as FP2 becomes dysregulated (increased beta wave activity). We will look at two very simple techniques to use with clients in order to manage the increased wave activity: diaphragmatic breathing and a type of meditation called Kirtan Kriya. These two techniques work to decrease activity in the sympathetic nervous system and bring it back to the parasympathetic nervous system. Diaphragmatic breathing will decrease high beta wave activity and guided imagery techniques will induce an alpha state that leads to a calm focus.

Diaphragmatic Breathing

Step 1: First, put one hand on your chest and one on your stomach or diaphragm, just below your rib cage. Notice which hand is moving the most. If it is your chest, you are probably not getting enough oxygen to your lungs, heart, and brain, unknowingly triggering a stress response. If it is your diaphragm, you are likely a healthy breather, but may need to reduce the number of breaths you take in a minute (Chapin & Russell-Chapin, 2014).

Step 2: Count the number of breaths you take each minute (in and out). Fifteen to 25 is too many, 12 to 15 average, and four to eight is optimum.

Step 3: With your hands still in place, breathe in and allow the air to expand your diaphragm, while keeping your chest relatively still. When full, hold your breath slightly before exhaling.

Step 4: Now exhale until all of the air is out of your lungs. If you can still talk, there is still more air to exhale. Again, pause once it is out before inhaling.

Step 5: Again, count the number of breaths you take each minute when focusing on diaphragmatic breathing. Remember, optimal relaxation is between four and six breaths per minute.

Step 6: Practice diaphragmatic breathing 15 minutes a day during daylight, active hours, versus a time when you are already relaxed.

Step 7: Strategically place reminder stickers, notes, messages, trinkets, etc. around to remind you to breathe intentionally and diaphragmatically.

Length of intervention: 10–15 minutes

Kirtan Kriya meditation

Kirtan Kriya is an ancient yoga and meditative practice that originated in India. This practice engages many areas of the brain due to the different pieces of the meditation including singing or chanting, finger movements (mudras), visualization, and sequence tracking. According to Khalsa and Newberg (2011), this type of yoga meditation has been shown to have several benefits with repeated practice including improved blood flow to the brain, increased brainwave activity in the frontal lobe, replenished acetylcholine, norepinephrine, and dopamine, increased energy levels and sleep quality, and reduced cortisol levels (Figure 4.4).

Step 1: Sit comfortably with your feet flat on the floor or in a comfortable yoga pose with legs crossed. Sit up straight and breathe normally with eyes closed if comfortable doing so.

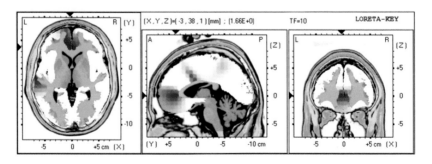

Figure 4.4 LORETA images of FP2 during Kirtan Kriya meditation intervention (along with FP1 and T3)

Step 2: Breathe in and out a few times to slow down your breathing pattern to a comfortable and relaxing pace.

Step 3: Begin by softly chanting "Saa, Taa, Naa, Maa."

Step 4: Add finger movements by touching your thumbs to each of your fingers with each chant. Touch your thumbs and index fingers as you say "Saa," your thumbs and middle fingers as you say "Taa," etc.

Step 5: Begin by chanting the sounds out loud for approximately two minutes. Then whisper softly for two minutes. Next, say the sound silently to yourself for four minutes. Whisper the sounds for two minutes again. Finally, chant out loud again for two minutes, for a total of 12 minutes.

Step 6. Finally, when the exercise is completed, inhale deeply, stretch your arms and hands above your head, and then lower them down each side as you exhale.

Length of intervention: 10–15 minutes

Conclusions

Chapter 4 explores the prefrontal cortex and the executive functions that help us to control our attention, decrease or eliminate unwanted behavior, and engage in planning, organization, and effective decision making. For each of the two sites, FP1 and FP2, dysregulation factors and two neurocounseling techniques were presented, as well as LORETA image activations for each site. FP1 neurocounseling techniques, with included step-by-step instructions, are reframing and task breakdown/planning. FP2 neurocounseling techniques, with included step-by-step instructions, are diaphragmatic breathing and Kirtan Kriya meditation.

References

Bell, A.C. & D'Zurilla, T.J. (2009). Problem-solving therapy for depression: A meta-analysis. *Clinical Psychology Review* 29(4), 348–353.

Bloom, L. & Bloom, C. (2007). Reframing: The transformative power of suffering. *Psychology Today*. Retrieved from www.psychologytoday.com/us/blog/stronger-the-broken-places/201712/reframing.

Bridgett, D.J., Burt, N.M., Edwards, E.S. & Deater-Deckard, K. (2015). Intergenerational transmission of self-regulation: A multidisciplinary review and integrative conceptual framework. *Psychological Bulletin* 141(3), 602–654. http://doi.org/10.1037/a0038662.

Carter, R. (2019). *The Human Brain Book*. New York: DK Publishing.

Chapin, T.J. & Russell-Chapin, L.A. (2014). *Neurotherapy and Neurofeedback: Brain-based treatment for psychological and behavioral problems*. New York: Routledge.

Demos, J.N. (2005). *Getting Started with Neurofeedback*. New York: Norton.

Ivey, A., Bradford Ivey, M., Zalaquett, C. & Quirk, K. (2009) Counseling and neuroscience: The cutting edge of the coming decade. *Counseling Today*. Retrieved from: http://ct.counseling.org/2009/12/readeviewpointcounseling-neuroscience-the-cutting-edge-of-the-coming-decade.

Khalsa, D.S. & Newberg, A. (2011). Kirtan Kriya meditation: A promising technique for enhancing cognition in memory-impaired older adults. In *Enhancing Cognitive Fitness in Adults*, pp. 419–431. New York: Springer.

Nezu, A.M., Nezu, C.M. & D'Zurilla, T.J. (2006). *Problem-Solving Therapy: A positive approach to clinical intervention*. New York: Springer.

Russell-Chapin, L. & Chapin, T. (2020). Neuroscience and the brain: What mental health counselors need to know. In J.C. Watson & M.K. Schmit (eds.) *Introduction to Clinical Mental Health Counseling*, p. 305. Los Angeles: SAGE.

Swingle, P.G. (2008). *Biofeedback for the Brain*. New Brunswick, NJ: Rutgers University.

Villines, Z. (2017). *Frontal Lobe: Functions, structure, and damage*. Retrieved from www.medicalnewstoday.com/articles/318139.php.

5

FRONTAL LOBES (F3, FZ, F4, F7, AND F8)

Seeing the Trees and Seeing the Forest for the Trees

Jason DeFord, Mary Bartido, and Tamika Lampkin

The efficiency and efficacy of the frontal lobes (F3, FZ, F4, F7, and F8) are essential to our everyday functioning and decision making. John McCrone (1991) brilliantly stated that "the brain is designed to grab what input it can and then boil it up into a froth of understanding." When the frontal lobes are regulated and connected to other parts of the brain, healthy behaviors occur. Life is much more easily engaged. In order to understand how the frontal lobes work individually and together, each location and function will be analyzed.

F3 Location and Function

The F3 function is located in the left hemisphere of the frontal lobe on the frontal cortex (Figure 5.1). According to Carter (2014), "the frontal cortex is responsible for abstract reasoning, conscious thought

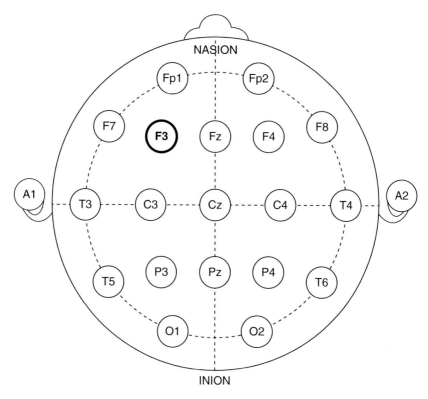

Figure 5.1 Head map graphic highlighting F3 site

and emotion, planning, and organization" (p. 138). More specifically, at the F3 location functions include "motor planning, right upper extremities control, right fine-motor coordination, visual episodic retrieval, mood elevation, object processing, emotional interpretation, and positive mood" (Chapin & Russell-Chapin, 2014). As noted in other chapters involving frontal lobe locations, this is an area that will interact with the amygdala as part of the social brain, as well as controlling our executive functions. At this spot we are better able to interpret others' emotions in working with the amygdala to create a sense of empathy, as well as a sense of self in a social context. When regulated, a positive sense of self leads to a more positive outlook and social awareness.

Implications of Dysregulation

In order to effectively help our clients, it is important to understand how the symptoms they are experiencing can be associated with a certain dysregulation in the brain. To get an accurate depiction of what the dysregulation is, a 19-channel EEG may be needed. This may not always be possible though, and therefore we can look at commonly identified symptoms and clinical implications of dysregulation at F3 as related to what brainwave functions may be affected. Two brainwave bands that we think about in relation to dysregulation at F3 are theta and beta. Theta waves are typically noted to be between 3 and 7 Hz (Swingle, 2008) and at the high end are related to reduced activity and involved in global thinking, spontaneity, daydreams, inattention, absence of directed thought, and meditation, while the lower end is related to depression, anxiety, and drowsiness (Chapin & Russell-Chapin, 2014). Beta waves are typically noted to be between 16 and 25 Hz (lobeta) and 28 and 40 Hz (hibeta) and related to information processing and problem solving (Swingle, 2008), as well as focus, analysis, relaxed thinking, and external orientation (Demos, 2005). When dysregulation is noted in a person at F3, depression and decreased executive functioning are often related to an increase in theta waves. When beta wave dysregulation is identified, an increase in activity can lead to obsessive-compulsive disorder (OCD). As we look to better inform and aid in regulation of the F3 location/function for our clients, interventions to support depression and executive functioning will be explored.

Two Neurocounseling Interventions

As noted previously, depression is one of the main concerns we as counselors will run into when looking at dysregulation at the F3 site. In order to better help our clients who are seeking help combatting the symptoms associated with this, we will explore two interventions: gratitude journaling and ANT therapy.

Gratitude Journaling

Having a sense of gratitude has long been understood to boost our mood and make us feel happier, though may not always be thought of as an intervention in the treatment of depression. According to Emmons and Stern (2013), gratitude has one of the strongest links to mental health and satisfaction with life of any personality trait – more so than even optimism, hope, or compassion. In addition, Petrocchi and Couyoumdjian (2016) found that the grateful disposition represents a protective factor against depression partly because it is significantly connected to lower levels of feelings of inadequacy, self-denigration, self-hate, and self-repugnance. Although a gratitude journal will be more effective when used outside a session as well, learning how to appropriately identify things we are grateful for in a session will help foster the changes.

Step 1: The counselor should help the client to be present and relaxed by using relaxation and grounding techniques (i.e., deep breathing, progressive muscle relaxation, etc.) in order to foster a more open mind.

Step 2: Encourage the client to write out five things that they feel grateful for. Focusing on a specific person can have more of an effect than things they are grateful for. Identifying surprises or unexpected events may have more of an emotional impact as well.

Step 3: Reflect and process these five things with the client. Encourage them to be as specific as possible and add as much detail as they can.

Step 4: Encourage continued use of the gratitude journal, especially in the morning and/or night to foster a sense of positivity and lightness. Length of intervention: 20–30 minutes

ANT Therapy

Automatic Negative Thought (ANT) therapy is a term coined by Dr. Daniel Amen in the early 1990s as a way to help his clients understand that their brains had become "infested by negative thoughts that were robbing them of their joy and stealing their happiness" (Amen, 2016). He indicates that when we have a negative thought, our brain produces negative chemicals that make us feel bad, both mentally and physically. When we have positive thoughts, the opposite happens. As we learn to better challenge our thoughts, we tend to have more positive thoughts, or less distortions, and therefore feel better (Figure 5.2).

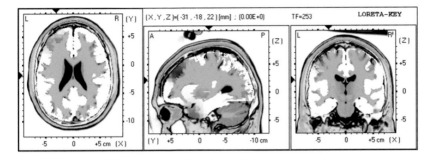

Figure 5.2 LORETA scans of F3 during ANT intervention (along with temporal lobe activation)

Step 1: Explain to the client how negative thoughts lead to negative chemicals being released and positive thoughts lead to positive chemicals being released. In addition, explain that as we get more negative thoughts, it becomes harder to challenge and get rid of them, and therefore we need to challenge thoughts as they come.

Step 2: Identify and explain common types of ANTs, or cognitive distortions. These include, but are not limited to, all-or-nothing thinking, black and white thinking, focusing only on negatives, fortune telling, mind reading, guilty feelings (should, must, have to, etc. thoughts), labeling, and blaming.

Step 3: Have your client identify a negative thought they have and work to identify which type of ANT it is and how to challenge/get rid of that ANT into a more positive or productive message.

Step 4: Encourage your client to keep track of their ANTs and learn to challenge them as they come, rather than waiting until they have built up and it is harder to move forward (Figure 5.3).

Length of intervention: 30–50 minutes

F4 Location and Function

The F4 function is located in the right hemisphere of the frontal lobe on the frontal cortex (Figure 5.4). According to Carter (2019), the frontal cortex is mostly responsible for abstract reasoning, conscious thought and emotion, planning, and organization. More specifically at the F4 location, functions include motor planning, left upper extremities control, left fine-motor coordination, verbal episodic and semantic retrieval, and regulation

AMEN CLINICS
Kill the ANTs Worksheet:

When you notice an ANT:
1. Write it down.
2. Identify the type of ANT it is.
3. Kill the ANT by talking back to it—challenge the thought!

What's your ANT?

_____

_____

What type of ANT is it?

_____

Kill the ANT by talking back to it:

_____

_____

_____

What's your ANT?

_____

_____

What type of ANT is it?

_____

Kill the ANT by talking back to it:

_____

_____

_____

Figure 5.3 Kill the ANTs worksheet

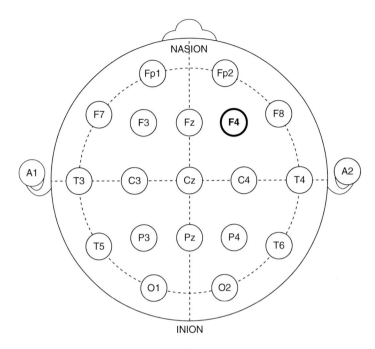

Figure 5.4 Head map graphic highlighting F4 site

of attention/impulse (Chapin & Russell-Chapin, 2014). As noted in other chapters involving frontal lobe locations, this is an area that will interact with the amygdala as part of the social brain, as well as controlling our executive functions. At this spot we are better able to control impulsive behaviors and speak with more concise thoughts and semantics.

Implications of Dysregulation

In order to effectively help our clients, it is important to understand how the symptoms they are experiencing can be associated with a certain dysregulation in the brain. To get an accurate depiction of what the dysregulation is, a 19-channel EEG may be needed. This may not always be possible though, and therefore we can look at commonly identified symptoms and clinical implications of dysregulation at F4 as related to what brainwave functions may be affected. Two brainwave bands that we think about in relation to dysregulation at F4 are theta and beta. Theta waves are typically noted to be between 3 and 7 Hz (Swingle,

2008) and at the high end are related to reduced activity and involved in global thinking, spontaneity, daydreams, inattention, absence of directed thought, and meditation, while the lower end is related to depression, anxiety, and drowsiness (Chapin & Russell-Chapin, 2014). Beta waves are typically noted to be between 16 and 25 Hz (lobeta) and 28 and 40 Hz (hibeta) and related to information processing and problem solving (Swingle, 2008), as well as focus, analysis, relaxed thinking, and external orientation (Demos, 2005). When dysregulation is noted in a person at F4, lack of tact, disorganized dialogue, and poor use of analogy and irony are often related to an increase in theta waves. When beta wave dysregulation is identified, an increase in activity can lead to hypervigilance. As we look to better inform and aid in regulation of the F4 location/function for our clients, interventions to better manage motor planning activities and increase verbal episodic and semantic retrieval will be explored.

Two Neurocounseling Interventions

In order to activate appropriate brainwave activity at F4, visualization exercises and analogy completion exercises will be explored as a means to encourage motor planning and verbal retrieval.

Visualization

Visualization exercise, or mental practice, has long been recognized as a beneficial activity to aid in motor performance without the use of physical activity. Even as far back as in 1983, Feltz & Landers noted that mental practice improves motor performance for athletes, with other research studies continuing to showcase this benefit in other motor skills. Bernardi et al. (2013) identify that for musicians mental practice can be effectively used to rehearse and practice complex motor sequences in the music domain. They also stated that it is linked to increased movement velocity which supports the idea that motor imagery might improve movement control (Figure 5.5).

Step 1: Ask your client to sit in a relaxing position, and if comfortable doing so, close their eyes. Begin working on slowing down breathing through use of diaphragmatic breathing.

Step 2: As your client relaxes, ask them to begin picturing themselves in the arena in which they would be participating (i.e., golf course, orchestra, dance floor, etc.). Encourage them to be as specific as possible, using all of their senses to really place themselves in that setting.

Step 3: After a few minutes of allowing the client to be in the setting, ask them to experience their task at hand. Encourage them to "feel" the emotions associated with the task before, during, and after it is accomplished. Again, encourage use of all the senses.

Step 4: As the task has been accomplished, allow the client to open their eyes if closed, and process the experience. What went well and where might there have been struggles to stay focused. Encourage practice outside the session as well.

Length of intervention: 20–30 minutes

Analogy Completion

As noted previously, an increase in theta waves at the F4 location may cause problems with verbal episodic and semantic memory retrieval, such as struggling to use analogies and irony in an appropriate manner. There have been many studies detailing the differences between episodic and semantic memory, dating back to the introduction of these concepts in 1972 (Tulving, 1972). Since then, other researchers have identified that there are many different areas of the brain that are involved in the memory process, including Binder & Desai (2011), who note that with semantic memory, there is participation of modality-specific sensory, motor, and emotion systems in language comprehension, and the

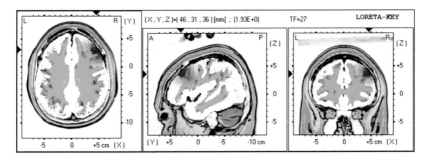

Figure 5.5 LORETA scans of F4 during visualization intervention

existence of large brain regions that participate in comprehension tasks but are not modality-specific. As a way in which to benefit short-term memory and analogous recall, we will explore the memory game.

Step 1: Prior to beginning this exercise, make notecards with one analogy broken up and put on two separate cards. Lay out the cards face down in a grid so the client must pick one at a time and flip it over, then try and find the completion to the analogy on another card.

Step 2: As the client flips over the first card, ask them to form a completion to the analogy on their own, prior to trying to finding the other card that fits. For example, the client flips over "puppy is to dog" and they may say "as kitten is to cat."

Step 3: Continue to play until all of the analogies are completed and matched. The client must come up with new examples each time a card is flipped.

Length of intervention: 30–50 minutes

FZ Location and Function

The FZ location is on the midline of the frontal cortex of the brain in the front of the head (Figure 5.6). According to Carter (2014), the frontal cortex is responsible for abstract reasoning, conscious thought and emotion, planning, and organization. More specifically at the FZ location, functions include motor planning of both lower extremities and midline, running, walking, kicking, response and emotional inhibition, and grooming (Chapin & Russell-Chapin, 2014). As this site is located on the midline of the brain, FZ will interact closely with the rest of the brain, especially as it relates to introspection of self and others within the default mode network (DMN). According to Russell-Chapin et al. (2013), the DMN is a network of brain regions that help us process our internal, reflective world and the world of self and others. This network includes the medial orbital prefrontal cortex, the anterior cingulate, the posterior cingulate, the precuneus region, the inferior parietal lobes, and the hippocampus.

Implications of Dysregulation

Neurological dysregulation results when the brain is using the wrong brainwave, at the wrong time, for the wrong task. This causes a state of neurological over-arousal, under-arousal, or unstable arousal (Russell-Chapin & Chapin, 2011). To get an accurate depiction of what the dysregulation is, a 19-channel EEG may be needed. This may not always be possible though, and therefore we can look at commonly identified symptoms and clinical implications of dysregulation at FZ as related to what brainwave functions may be affected. Two brainwave bands that we think about in relation to dysregulation at FZ are theta and beta. Theta waves are typically noted to be between 3 and 7 Hz (Swingle, 2008) and at the high end are related to reduced activity and involved in global thinking, spontaneity, daydreams, inattention, absence of directed thought, and meditation, while the lower end is related to depression, anxiety, and drowsiness (Chapin & Russell-Chapin, 2014). Beta waves are typically noted to be between 16 and 25 Hz (lobeta) and 28 and 40 Hz (hibeta) and related to information processing and problem solving (Swingle, 2008), as well as focus, analysis, relaxed thinking, and external orientation (Demos, 2005). According to Chapin and Russell-Chapin (2014), when dysregulation happens in the FZ area of the brain it may cause increased beta and increased theta waves. Increased beta waves in the FZ brain area can cause disorders such as obsessive-compulsive disorder (OCD) and attention and motivation problems. Increased theta can lead to attention deficit hyperactivity disorder (ADHD) combined type.

Two Neurological Interventions

As noted previously, obsessive compulsive disorder (OCD) is often a diagnosis that comes from dysregulation at the FZ site. OCD is a common, chronic, and long-lasting disorder in which a person has uncontrollable, reoccurring thoughts (obsessions) and behaviors (compulsions) that he or she feels the urge to repeat over and over (National Institute of Mental Health, 2019). The stress and anxiety that is caused by OCD makes neurocounseling a great choice for clients who want to gain control. The first technique that will be explored is mindful meditation and the second will be heart rate variability.

Mindful Meditation

Mindful meditation is a neurocounseling approach that focuses on having clients enter a relaxed state by focusing on breathing. Research has shown

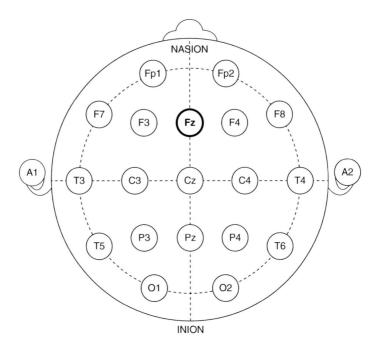

Figure 5.6 Head map graphic highlighting FZ site

mindfulness meditation to be very effective in helping clients who suffer from PTSD, trauma, and behavior and emotional issues (Wayne, 2018). A study performed by Hanstede, Gordon & Nyklicek (2008) on 17 adults, found 60% of participants had decreased symptoms of OCD once the study was completed.

Step 1: Have your client sit either in a chair with both feet touching the floor, or in a yoga pose on the floor with legs crossed.

Step 2: Ask your client to sit up straight and place their hands comfortably in their laps with arms parallel to their upper body. Have them drop their chin and let their gaze fall gently downward or close their eyes if that feels comfortable.

Step 3: Ask your client to begin to pay attention to their breathing, focusing on breathing in and out and the physical sensations that come with it (i.e., air moving through nose and/or mouth, belly rising and falling, etc.).

Step 4: Ask your client to identify when their mind wanders away from the breathing process and gently bring it back. They should be intentional in movements needed such as adjusting the body or scratching an itch, and take a second between noticing the urge and doing so.

Step 5: After 10–15 minutes of practicing this, ask your client to gently raise their gaze and notice what is going on in the environment around them and how they feel. Ask them to notice their thoughts and emotions and identify what they would like to do next.

Length of intervention: 20–30 minutes

Heart Rate Variability

Heart rate variability (HRV) is an effective biofeedback technique that utilizes heart rhythm feedback to promote self-regulation. It measures the normally occurring beat-to-beat changes in heart rate. According to McCraty (2016), an optimal level of HRV within an organism reflects healthy function and an inherent self-regulatory capacity, adaptability, and resilience. When looking at heart rhythm patterns, emotional stress often leads to more erratic and irregular patterns as compared to positive emotions that lead to more smooth and wavelike patterns (Figure 5.7).

Note: In order to accurately measure HRV, additional equipment is needed to measure these patterns, though not necessarily essential to create true coherence through HRV training. There are many different companies and apps that provide HRV monitoring.

Step 1: Encourage your client to sit comfortably and begin to slow down their breathing. Good HRV coherence comes not only from a relaxed breathing pattern, but more so from actively engaging in a positive feeling.

Step 2: Heart Focus. Help your client focus their attention in the area of the heart, in the center of their chest.

Step 3: Heart Breathing. Continue to focus attention to the heart, and ask the client to imagine their breath going in and out through the heart.

Step 4: Heart Feeling. Encourage your client to try to feel a positive feeling. Encourage your client to think about a feeling of care for someone or something, or a feeling of appreciation for the good things in their life.

Step 5: While practicing these steps, encourage your client to keep a smooth, rhythmic breathing pattern. If using additional equipment

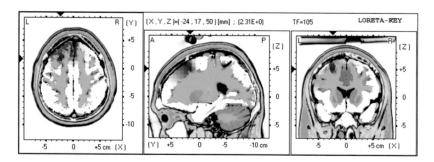

Figure 5.7 LORETA scans of FZ during HRV intervention

or apps, there is likely a guide for effective breathing patterns to follow along with.

Length of intervention: 10–15 minutes

F7 Location and Function

The F7 function is located in the left hemisphere of the frontal lobe on the frontal cortex (Figure 5.8). According to Carter (2014), the frontal cortex is responsible for abstract reasoning, conscious thought and emotion, planning, and organization. More specifically, at the F7 location functions include "verbal expression, speech fluency, cognitive mood regulation, visual and auditory working memory, attentional gate and Broca's area" (Chapin & Russell-Chapin, 2014). As noted in other chapters involving frontal lobe locations, this is an area that will interact with the amygdala as part of the social brain, as well as controlling our executive functions. At this spot we often look to focus on speech within Broca's area. According to Johns Hopkins (2015), Broca's area is most active during word formulation before speech occurs, and is a major component of a complex speech network, which also involves Wernicke's area for matching sounds to their meanings.

Implications of Dysregulation

In order to effectively help our clients, it is important to understand how the symptoms they are experiencing can be associated with a certain dysregulation in the brain. To get an accurate depiction of what the dysregulation is, a 19-channel EEG may be needed. This may not always

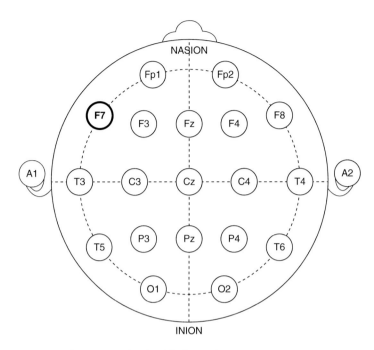

Figure 5.8 Head map graphic highlighting F7 site

be possible though, and therefore we can look at commonly identified symptoms and clinical implications of dysregulation at F7 as related to what brainwave functions may be affected. Two brainwave bands that we think about in relation to dysregulation at F7 are theta and beta. Theta waves are typically noted to be between 3 and 7 Hz (Swingle, 2008) and at the high end are related to reduced activity and involved in global thinking, spontaneity, daydreams, inattention, absence of directed thought, and meditation, while the lower end is related to depression, anxiety, and drowsiness (Chapin & Russell-Chapin, 2014). Beta waves are typically noted to be between 16 and 25 Hz (lobeta) and 28 and 40 Hz (hibeta) and related to information processing and problem solving (Swingle, 2008), as well as focus, analysis, relaxed thinking, and external orientation (Demos, 2005). When dysregulation is noted in a person at F7, speech and word-finding problems are often related to an increase in theta waves. When beta wave dysregulation is identified, an increase in activity can lead to input control. Damage or dysregulation to Broca's area can cause issues putting thoughts into words, difficulty monitoring what is said, trouble with making corrections or adjusting flow of speech, and even completing sentences (Johns Hopkins, 2015).

Two Neurocounseling Interventions

In order to assist clients who may have brain dysregulation in the F7 area, there are many techniques that are applicable during counseling sessions to help regulate brain function. Again, as this is the part of the brain that holds Broca's area, we will look at how neurocounseling techniques that help with speech can help to regulate activity here. Phonological components analysis and response elaboration training therapy are two techniques that will be described for use with these clients.

Phonological Components Analysis

According to Marcotte et al. (2018), phonological components analysis is a sound-based therapy in which participants are asked to identify five phonological components of a word they cannot name, guided by the use of a chart. This treatment will help in dealing with speech issues related to Broca's aphasia. According to Leonard, Rochon & Laird (2008), seven of ten people in their study benefited from this training, including maintenance of gains and showing some generalization to untrained words. In addition, van Hees et al. in 2013 indicated that seven of eight participants showed significant improvements in naming items, with six of seven maintaining at follow-up.

Step 1: Place a picture of an object in the center of a chart and ask the client to name the picture.

Step 2: Ask the client to answer five phonological questions related to that picture: what sound does it start with, what other words start with the same sound, what sound does it end with, what does this rhyme with, and how many beats does the word have.

Step 3: Ask the client to name the picture again, reviewing the phonological questions again if needed, and then name the picture with the client.

Step 4: Repeat these steps with different pictures.

Length of intervention: 30–50 minutes

Phonological components analysis

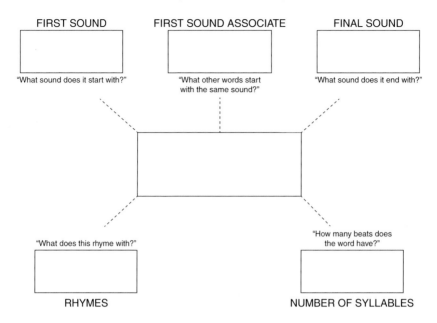

Phonological components analysis

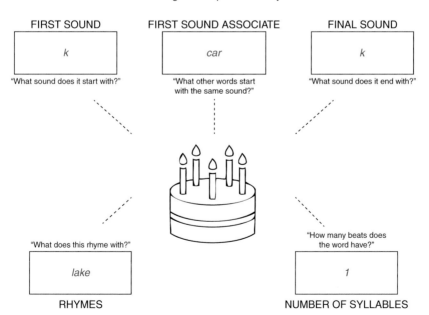

Response Elaboration Training

Response elaboration training was first introduced by Dr. Kevin Kearns (Kearns, 1983), and has been modified since then to be more efficient. This technique is used to "increase the number of content words in spontaneous speech for people with aphasia" (Sutton, 2019). It is not a therapy that has right or wrong answers, but rather asks the clients to use more words to describe the actions they see as compared to baseline measures (Figure 5.9).

Step 1: Show your client a picture of a person completing an action and ask them to describe the picture. Take note of the number of descriptive words used in their response.

Step 2: Positively reinforce the response, while adding an even more complete version of the description.

Step 3: Ask an appropriate follow-up question (who, what, where, when, why, how) to get more information from the client. Again take note of the amount and different descriptive words used by the client.

Step 4: Combine the responses and say the new sentence. Ask the client to repeat it back to you.

Step 5: Show the original picture and ask the client to describe what is happening in it again, just as in step 1. Compare the number of descriptor words as compared to the first time. Repeat for different action pictures.

Length of intervention: 30–50 minutes

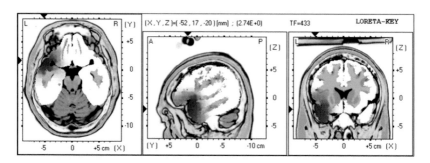

Figure 5.9 LORETA scans during response elaboration training

F8 Location and Function

The F8 function is located in the right hemisphere of the frontal lobe (Figure 5.10). Kolb and Whishaw (2009) noted the majority of the tissue of the frontal lobe comprises the front of the central sulcus. This area is 20% of the neocortex and is broken into three sections: motor, premotor, and prefrontal. The functions of these areas are as follows: the motor cortex is responsible for making movements, while the premotor cortex selects the movements (Kolb & Whishaw, 2009, p. 396). The prefrontal cortex controls the cognitive processes. This will allow the correct movements to be made at the correct time and place, and these specific selections of movements are made through external or internal cues, self-knowledge, or made in response to something. The functions of F8 are the following: emotional expression, drawing, endogenous mood regulation, face recognition, emotional processing, visual/spatial working memory, and sustained attention (Chapin & Russell-Chapin, 2014).

Implications of Dysregulation

In order to effectively help our clients, it is important to understand how the symptoms they are experiencing can be associated with a certain dysregulation in the brain. To get an accurate depiction of what the dysregulation is, a 19-channel EEG may be needed. This may not always be possible though, and therefore we can look at commonly identified symptoms and clinical implications of dysregulation at F8 as related to what brainwave functions may be affected. Two brainwave bands that we think about in relation to dysregulation at F8 are theta and beta. Theta waves are typically noted to be between 3 and 7 Hz (Swingle, 2008) and at the high end are related to reduced activity and involved in global thinking, spontaneity, daydreams, inattention, absence of directed thought, and meditation, while the lower end is related to depression, anxiety, and drowsiness (Chapin & Russell-Chapin, 2014). Beta waves are typically noted to be between 16 and 25 Hz (lobeta) and 28 and 40 Hz (hibeta) and related to information processing and problem solving (Swingle, 2008), as well as focus, analysis, relaxed thinking, and external orientation (Demos, 2005). If a person has excess theta wave frequencies, this person is susceptible to a lack of prosody, and if there are excessive

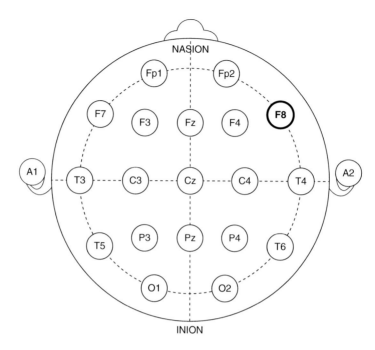

Figure 5.10 Head map graphic highlighting F8 site

beta wave frequencies, this person is likely to be oversensitive to the speech intonation of others. Other F8 functions which become affected are endogenous mood regulation, emotional expression, and emotional processing, which can all be seen in disruptive mood dysregulation disorder (DMDD).

The right frontal area (F8) is activated while other areas, especially the left hemisphere, is underactivated.

Two Neurocounseling Interventions

Sleep Hygiene/Lavender Relaxation

One way to help regulate theta frequencies, and therefore help mood regulation, is through establishing proper sleep hygiene. One assessment a clinician can use to help determine a person's sleep hygiene is through the Adolescent Sleep Hygiene Scale (ASHS). The ASHS is a self-report questionnaire that assesses theoretically based sleep hygiene domains that influence the sleep quality and quantity of youth aged 12 years or older (Storfer-Isser et al., 2013). The following are suggested steps to take in establishing proper sleep hygiene as suggested by Irish et al. (2015): avoid caffeine, avoid nicotine, avoid alcohol, exercise regularly, manage stress, reduce bedroom noise, sleep timing regularity, and avoid daytime naps. As managing stress seems to be a broad suggestion, we will look at how lavender oil may help to initiate a relaxation response that will aid in better sleep patterns. Lavender has been proven to help with relaxation by increasing the power of theta and alpha brain activities in all brain regions, as well as decreasing the arousal level of the automatic nervous system (ANS) (Sayorwan et al., 2012) (Figure 5.11).

Note: It is important to read warning labels and have a properly diluted mixture when using oils on skin as it could become irritated.

Step 1: Gauge your client's stress level by asking them to identify where they are by a number between one and ten, with ten being the most stressed they've ever felt.

Step 2: Ask your client to sit in a comfortable position and begin to slow down their breathing.

Step 3: Either offer to roll on the diluted lavender mixture, or allow the client to take several deep breaths in of the lavender.

Step 4: Encourage the client to be in the present, noticing the smell, and relaxing more as they take each breath.

Step 5: After several minutes and cycles of breath, ask your client to identify on the scale of one to ten again where their stress level is at this time.

Length of intervention: 10–15 minutes

Mindfully Eating

The second approach to consider is based on mindfulness-focused practices; this will help with the excessive beta frequencies which result in anger, irritability, and emotional dysregulation. Mindfulness-based interventions can assist in emotional regulation by developing skills that maintain an open and accepting attitude toward experience, which is a key factor in emotion regulation and affective outcomes (Chiodelli et al., 2018). According to Davis & Hayes (2011), research has illustrated the ability of mindfulness meditation to enhance emotional regulation by eliciting

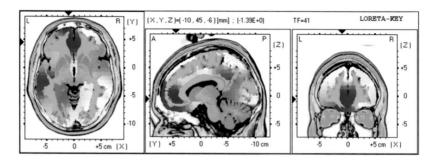

Figure 5.11 LORETA image of F8 during lavendar intervention

positive emotions, minimizing negative affect and rumination, and enabling effective emotion regulation. Mindfulness meditation can also help develop skills of self-observation and allows for a present-moment input to be integrated in a novel way (Davis & Hayes, 2011). However, there are other methods that a person can use to be mindful, such as the raisin exercise as described by Brown, Marquis & Guiffrida (2013).

> Step 1: Provide your client with a raisin and ask them to focus their consciousness on the sight and texture of the raisin, then eventually the smell and taste.
>
> Step 2: Once they have chewed and swallowed the raisin, ask them to be aware of the sensations the raisin has as it travels down their throat and into their stomach.
>
> Step 3: Remind your client that drifting thoughts are normal and to acknowledge this fact without any judgment, but then refocus and return back to the physical experience of the exercise.
>
> Step 4: Continuously practice this exercise or other mindfulness-based interventions with intentional awareness and eventually mindfulness will become habitual.
>
> Length of intervention: 10–15 minutes

Conclusions

Chapter 5 explores the frontal lobes, which help us to see details and data of our world (left side), as well as seeing the bigger picture and synthesizing the smaller pieces of information (right side). For each of the five sites, F3, F4, FZ, F7, and F8, dysregulation factors and two neurocounseling techniques were presented, as well as LORETA image activations for each site.

References

Amen, D.G. (2016). Amen Clinics ANT therapy. *The Amen Clinics Method Toolbox: Forms, questionnaires, and planning tools to improve diagnosis and outcomes for those you serve.* MindWorks Innovations, Inc.

Bernardi, N.F., De Buglio, M., Trimarchi, P.D., Chielli, A. & Bricolo, E. (2013). Mental practice promotes motor anticipation: Evidence from skilled music performance. *Frontiers in Human Neuroscience* 7, 451. https://doi.org/10.3389/fnhum.2013.00451.

Binder, Jeffrey R. & Desai, Rutvik H. (2011). The neurobiology of semantic memory. *Trends in Cognitive Sciences* 15(11), 527–536. DOI:10.1016/j.tics.2011.10.001.

Brown, A.P., Marquis, A. & Guiffrida, D.A. (2013). Mindfulness-based interventions in counseling. *Journal of Counseling and Development* 91(1), 96–104. http://dx.doi.org.ezproxy.bradley.edu/10.1002/j.1556-6676.2013.00077.x

Carter, R. (2019). *The Human Brain Book* (2nd ed). New York: DK Publishing.

Carter, R. (2014). *The Human Brain Book.* New York: DK Publishing.

Chapin, T.J. & Russell-Chapin, L. (2014). *Neurotherapy and Neurofeedback: Brain-based treatment for psychological and behavioral problems.* New York: Routledge.

Chiodelli, R., Mello, L.T.N., Jesus, S.N. & Andretta, I. (2018). Effects of a brief mindfulness-based intervention on emotional regulation and levels of mindfulness in senior students. *Psicologia: Reflexão e Crítica* 31, 10. http://dx.doi.org.ezproxy.bradley.edu/10.1186/s41155-018-0099-7.

Davis, D.M. & Hayes, A.J. (2011). What are the benefits of mindfulness? A practice review of psychotherapy-related research. *Psychotherapy* 48(2), 198–208. DOI:10.1037/a0022062.

Demos, J.N. (2005). *Getting Started with Neurofeedback.* New York: Norton.

Emmons, R.A. & Stern, R. (2013). Gratitude as a psychotherapeutic intervention. *Journal of Clinical Psychology* 69(8), 846–855.

Feltz, D.L. & Landers, D. (1983). The effects of mental practice on motor skill learning and performance: A meta analysis. *Journal of Sport Psychology* 5, 25–57.

Hanstede, M., Gordon, Y. & Nyklicek, I. (2008). The effects of a mindfulness intervention on obsessive-compulsive symptoms in a non-clinical student population. *Journal of Nervous and Mental Disease* 196(10), 776–779. DOI:10.1097/NMD.0b013e31818786b8.

Irish, L.A., Kline, C.E., Gunn, H.E., Buysse, D.J. & Hall, M.H. (2015). The role of sleep hygiene in promoting public health: A review of empirical evidence. *Sleep Medicine Reviews* 22, 23–36. http://dx.doi.org.ezproxy.bradley.edu/10.1016/j.smrv.2014.10.001.

Johns Hopkins (2015). Broca's area is the brain's scriptwriter, shaping speech, study finds. *Johns Hopkins Medicine, News and Publications.* Retrieved from www.hopkinsmedicine.org/news/media/releases/brocas_area_is_the_brains_scriptwriter_shaping_speech_study_finds.

Kearns, K.P. (1983). Response elaboration training for patient initiated utterances. In R.H. Brookshire (ed), *Clinical Aphasiology*, pp. 196–204. Minneapolis, MN: BRK.

Kolb, B. & Whishaw, Q.I. (2009). The frontal lobes. In *The Fundamentals of Human Neuropsychology*. New York: Worth Publishers. Retrieved from http://192.168.1.1:8181/http://psych.colorado.edu/~campeaus/2022/K&WChap16.pdf.

Leonard, C., Rochon, E. & Laird, L. (2008). Treating naming impairments in aphasia: Findings from a phonological components analysis treatment. *Aphasiology* 22(9), 923–947. DOI:10.1080/02687030701831474.

Marcotte, Karine, Laird, Laura, Bitan, Tali, Meltzer, Jed A., Graham, Simon J., Leonard, Carol & Rochon, Elizabeth (2018). Therapy-induced neuroplasticity in chronic aphasia after phonological component analysis: A matter of intensity. *Frontiers in Neurology* 9. DOI:10.3389/fneur.2018.00225.

McCraty, R. (2016). Exploring the role of the heart in human performance: An overview of research conducted by the HeartMath Institute. In *Science of the Heart* (vol. 2). DOI:10.13140/RG.2.1.3873.5128.

McCrone, J. (1991). *The Ape that Spoke: Language and the evolution of the human mind.* New York: William Morrow.

National Institute of Mental Health (2019, October). Obsessive-compulsive disorder. Retrieved from www.nimh.nih.gov/health/topics/obsessive-compulsive-disorder-ocd/index.shtml.

Petrocchi, N. & Couyoumdjian, A. (2016). The impact of gratitude on depression and anxiety: The mediating role of criticizing, attacking, and reassuring the self. *Self and Identity* 15(2), 191–205.

Russell-Chapin, L. (2014). Neurocounseling: Bringing the brain into clinical practice. Retrieved from http://factbasedhealth.com/neurocounseling-bringing-brain-clinical-practice/.

Russell-Chapin, L., Kemmerly, T., Liu, W-C., Zagardo, M.T., Chapin, T., Dailey, D. & Dinh, D. (2013). The effects of neurofeedback in the default mode network: Pilot study results of medicated children with ADHD, *Journal of Neurotherapy* 75, 35–42.

Russell-Chapin, L.A. & Chapin, T.J. (2011). Neurofeedback: A third option when counseling and medication are not sufficient. Retrieved from http://counselingoutfitters.com/ vistas/vistas11/Article_48.pdf.

Sayorwan, W., Siripornpanich, V., Piriyapunyaporn, T., Hongratanaworakit, T., Kotchabhakdi, N. & Ruangrungsi, N. (2012). The effects of lavender oil inhalation on emotional states, autonomic nervous system, and brain electrical activity. *Journal of the Medical Assococation of Thailand* 95(4), 598–606. Retrieved from www.jmat.mat.or.th.

Storfer-Isser, A., Lebourgeois, M.K., Harsh, J., Tompsett, C.J. & Redline, S. (2013). Psychometric properties of the adolescent sleep hygiene scale. *Journal of Sleep Research* 22(6), 707–716. http://dx.doi.org.ezproxy.bradley.edu/10.1111/jsr.12059.

Swingle, P.G. (2008). *Biofeedback for the Brain*. New Brunswick, NJ: Rutgers University.

Sutton, M.S. (2019). How to: Response Elaboration Training (RET) for sentences in aphasia. Retrieved from https://tactustherapy.com/response-elaboration-training-ret/.

Tulving, E. (1972). Episodic and semantic memory. In E. Tulving & W. Donaldson, (eds.). *Organization of Memory*, pp. 381–403. New York,: Academic Press.

van Hees, S., Angwin, A., McMahon, K. & Copland, D. (2013). A comparison of semantic feature analysis and phonological components analysis for the treatment of naming impairments in aphasia. *Neuropsychological Rehabilitation* 23(1), 102–132. DOI:10.1080/09602011.2012.726201.

Wayne, T. (2018, April). Neurocounseling and trauma. Retrieved from www.crisisprevention.com/Blog/April-2016/Neurocounseling-and-Trauma.

6

SENSORY MOTOR (C3, CZ, AND C4)

Helping the World Move

Anna Clancy Resniak, Brooke Poling, and Leah Maloney

To better understand the location and function of the Sensory Motor Strip, the words of Tim Berners-Lee and Mark Fischetti (2000) help explain. These authors believe that "all we know and all we are, come from the way our neurons are connected." C3, CZ, and C4 locations certainly exemplify that very notion of needed motor skills and will be individually described.

C3 Location and Function

C3 communicates with many different parts of the brain, which leads it to being responsible for many different functions. Its biggest responsibility is for the sensorimotor integration of the right upper extremities, i.e., the right arm, hand, etc. In other words, C3 is responsible for the communication between the sensory system, or nerves, and the motor system, or muscles of the brain and the right upper extremities. C3 has also been tied to handwriting, short-term memory, and the alerting responses. C3

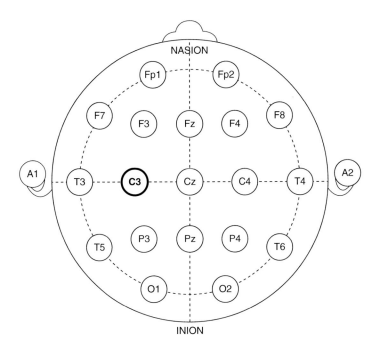

Figure 6.1 Head map graphic highlighting C3 site

is located in the frontal lobe between CZ and T3 (Figure 6.1). The frontal lobe is responsible for the everyday functions that allow us to successfully engage in independent and self-serving behaviors (Stuss, 2011). Needless to say, C3 is responsible for very important everyday tasks, which could lead to frustration and potential life alteration if a dysfunction were to occur.

Implications of Dysregulation

When dysregulation of C3 occurs, there is impaired sensorimotor integration in the client. Proper sensorimotor integration allows the client to respond appropriately with predicted sensory feedback and motor commands. For example, a properly functioning C3 would allow a message to be sent from the brain to the right hand if a person were to place their right hand on a hot surface, causing the person to immediately remove the hand from the hot surface. High levels of theta in C3 would be displayed in poor handwriting. High levels of beta in C3 would show as motor hyperactivity.

Damage to the frontal lobe, including traumatic brain injuries (TBIs), can result in dysregulation of C3. Diseases such as Parkinson's disease have also been tied to dysfunction in the frontal lobe, along with mental health issues such as attention deficit hyperactivity disorder (ADHD). When working with clients with the above-mentioned issues, it is important to be mindful of the symptoms of dysregulation of C3, such as sensory feedback and motor commands or delay in the alerting system. When dysregulation occurs in C3, the client can either be sped up or slowed down, which can also be seen in the emotional responses of the client. As mentioned above, high levels of beta in C3 appear as motor hyperactivity, such as that in those suffering from ADHD. Neuroimaging can be effective in diagnosing the dysregulation, while neurocounseling can be effective in overcoming the dysregulation.

Two Neurocounseling Interventions

Mindfulness Jar

One therapeutic technique option would be to use physical exercise/activity with motor hyperactivity. A fidget, something the client can hold in their hands while also talking with the therapist, would be a beneficial physical activity to assist with dysregulation of C3. Good examples of fidgets would be stress balls or a mindfulness jar. The idea of this jar is that each intense feeling lasts 60 seconds. When the client is feeling overwhelmed with a feeling, the mindfulness jar provides the act of shaking the jar, which addresses motor hyperactivity. It also teaches the client to wait for the glitter to all set at the bottom of the jar before acting impulsively. Step-by-step instructions for creating a mindfulness jar are as follows:

Step 1: Gather all of the necessary ingredients for the mindfulness jar (Mason jar, liquid glycerin, dish soap, hot water, glitter).

Step 2: Fill the Mason jar ¾ full with hot water. Drop in 2 tablespoons of liquid glycerin and a drop of dish soap. Close the lid to the jar and gently shake the ingredients together.

Step 3: Have the client pick at least three different colors of glitter to represent three strong emotions they feel frequently. (Example: red for anger, blue for sadness, orange for anxiety). Have the client place as much or as little of each glitter into the jar to represent these emotions.

Step 4: Have the client check to make sure the lid is tightly secure before gently shaking the Mason jar, paying attention to the movement of the glitter in the jar.

Step 5: Explain the experience to the client. Each strong emotion lasts on average 60 seconds. The goal of the mindfulness jar is to have the client actively shake the jar, being mindful of the way the "emotions" are moving throughout the jar. Encourage the client to wait until all of the glitter has settled to the bottom of the jar before making any decisions while experiencing these strong emotions. Encourage the client to also utilize the jar multiple times when needed.

Length of intervention: 30 minutes

Diaphragmatic Breathing

Dysregulation of C3 can affect the alerting response. Intervention options for issues with the alerting response would be diaphragmatic breathing and skin temperature training. Teaching clients how to breathe deeply through the diaphragm allows the chance to calm the alerting responses. Guided meditation techniques, as well as skin temperature training, allow an opportunity for the client to work on feeling safe and calm (Chapin & Russell-Chapin, 2014). These techniques can require practice at a clinical level with the client. These simple techniques can provide life-changing opportunities for clients to regain control over their own bodies. (Figure 6.2) Steps for diaphragmatic breathing techniques with a client are as follows:

Step 1: Create a safe space for the client. It is important that the client is invited to participate in a way that feels safe for them. Remind the client that they are in control of how this technique goes. Inform the client that if they become triggered in any way, they may inform the counselor that they need a break.

Step 2: Invite the client to close their eyes, again reminding the client that they are in a safe space.

Step 3: Invite the client to place their hands on their diaphragm. Explain to the client that this area can be found by placing their hands on their stomach, just under their ribs.

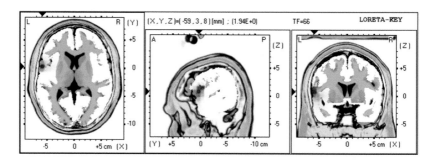

Figure 6.2 LORETA imaging for C3 during diaphragmatic breathing

Step 4: Ask the client to take a deep, ten-count breath in through the nose. Encourage the client to pay close attention to the movement of their hands resting lightly on their diaphragm.

Step 5: Ask the client to breathe out for ten counts through the mouth, again paying close attention to the movement of their hands on their diaphragm.

Step 6: Complete steps three through five for about ten minutes.

Step 7: Discuss with the client what they are feeling within their body. What did the client feel their hands doing as they were breathing? How was the client feeling prior to the deep breathing? How is the client feeling now?

Length of intervention: 10–20 minutes

CZ Location and Function

CZ is located in the center of the head at the midline (Figure 6.3). It is situated in the sensory and motor cortices, and is directly above the basal ganglia (Carter, 2014). The basal ganglia, sensory cortex, and motor cortex are integral for sensation and movement. Not surprisingly, CZ has functions that relate to sensations, movement, and motor control. Many of its functions are related to the integration of sensory input and motor output. Because CZ spans into both the frontal and parietal lobes, it is important for conscious thought and planning for motor movement, as well as sensory information and body position awareness. CZ is important for a person's sensorimotor rhythm and ability to coordinate sensory input with motor output and movements (Chapin & Russell-Chapin,

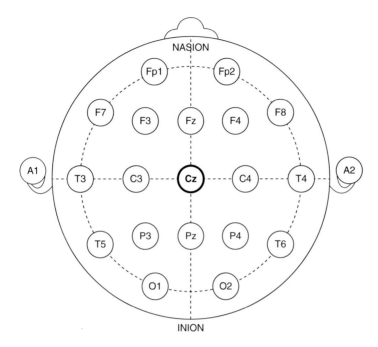

Figure 6.3 Head map graphic highlighting CZ site

2014). CZ also allows people to have awareness of their body position and movements.

Implications of Dysregulation

Dysregulation at CZ may present in a variety of forms, and clinicians may want to work with a client on regulating CZ when they notice difficulties integrating sensory input and motor output. Interventions to regulate CZ's brainwave activity can be useful for a variety of presenting concerns, including attention deficit hyperactivity disorder (ADHD), sensory motor disorders, attention and motivation difficulties, epilepsy, stroke, and paralysis (Chapin & Russell-Chapin, 2014). Improving brainwave regulation at CZ may also be beneficial for clients with headaches, migraines, chronic fatigue syndrome, Tourette's syndrome, Parkinson's, reactive attachment disorder, and restless leg symptoms (Collura & Frederick, 2017). Clients with the previously mentioned presenting problems may benefit from neurocounseling for CZ because there are related issues with sensory and motor areas of the brain, including areas such as the thalamus, sensory cortex, substantia nigra, and basal ganglia (Carter, 2014). Utilizing a client's ability to execute motor movements and improve sensorimotor rhythm will enable the client to improve their brainwave regulation at CZ.

There are multiple specific presenting concerns that have been related to dysregulation of brainwaves at CZ. An excess of theta waves at CZ is associated with ADHD (Chapin & Russell-Chapin, 2014). High beta levels at Cz are associated with attention and motivation difficulties (Chapin & Russell-Chapin, 2014). High beta may be associated with headaches and chronic fatigue syndrome (Collura & Frederick, 2017).

Two Neurocounseling Interventions

Neurocounseling interventions aimed to regulate brainwaves at CZ can include a variety of activities. Techniques should utilize sensorimotor integration and motor movement. Depending on the client's ability level and presenting concerns, the following techniques may not be appropriate. However, nearly any activity that requires the client to coordinate the sensory input they are receiving with their movements will utilize CZ.

Dancing

One technique to consider for helping clients to regulate brainwave activity at CZ is dancing. Dancing can be a fun way to encourage gross motor movement and incorporate sensory input with motor output. Dancing activates the sensory and motor cortices and requires mental coordination (Edwards, 2015). Research indicates that dance training improves sensorimotor skills, particularly whole-body movement (Karpati et al., 2016). Additionally, it can be enjoyable for the client and a way for clients with difficulty sustaining attention and/or sitting still to channel their energy. If the counselor is willing to dance with the client, it can increase the therapeutic rapport and show that the counselor is willing to practice the interventions that they are encouraging the client to perform.

Step 1: Counselors should allow the client to choose a song that they enjoy and would be willing to dance to.

Step 2: If possible, the counselor can have a dancing video game on their computer or a console in the office, because these video games are able to give the client immediate feedback through camera sensors on their accuracy of dance moves. Clients can follow the dancer on the screen and receive feedback on the accuracy of their sensorimotor rhythm and accuracy of integrating sensory input (i.e., the dance moves seen on the screen and the beat of the music) with their motor output.

Step 3: Another option is pulling up a video of the song on the computer. The client may prefer to have a video of someone dancing to the song (i.e., dancing tutorial) so they can follow along with the dance moves. Otherwise, the client can make up their own dance moves and express their creativity.

Step 4: If the client is not comfortable with dancing, have them choose a song and clap along, nod their head, or stomp their feet to the beat. This still requires the client to integrate sensory input with their motor output. Encourage the client to practice dancing or the alternate options at home at least a couple of times before the next session. Educate the client about why you are asking them to utilize this technique and how it relates to the concerns they have brought to counseling.

Length of intervention: 10 minutes

Puzzle

Another possible technique that can be useful in regulating brainwave activity at CZ is doing a puzzle, because it requires fine motor movement and sensory, spatial awareness. Jigsaw puzzling engages multiple aspects of cognition and long-term habits of doing puzzles can promote healthy visuospatial cognition (Fissler et al., 2018). Puzzles promote hand-eye coordination, motor skills, problem solving, and memory (Myers, 2011). Puzzles can be easily incorporated into a counseling session and can be a technique that the client can do at home as well (Figure 6.4).

Step 1: Have a variety of puzzles available depicting different scenes/pictures and various difficulty levels.

Step 2: Ensure that you have puzzles available that are appropriate for different ages, including young children. It may be beneficial to

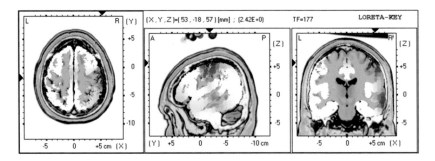

Figure 6.4 LORETA imaging for CZ during puzzle intervention (most evident in center image)

have adult puzzles with large pieces for clients with poor vision or difficulties with fine motor skills.

Step 3: The client can work on the puzzle during conversation in the session if they are able to maintain attention. If the client prefers to focus their full attention on the puzzle, the counselor can ask questions that encourage the client to attend to the puzzle. Examples can include "What colors do you see on the piece? Where might it fit? Can you find a similar-looking area on the puzzle box picture? Can you find all the corner and edge pieces?" By asking questions about the characteristics of the puzzle pieces, the client is attending to sensory information and planning and executing fine motor movements to put the pieces together.

Step 4: Explain to the client what fine motor movements are and how they are utilizing fine motor movements by doing a puzzle, as well as why working on a puzzle is helping them regulate their brain-wave activity at CZ and how regulation can benefit them.

Length of intervention: 15 minutes

C4 Location and Function

C4 is located in the central brain in the right hemisphere found behind the sulcus in the sensory area (Figure 6.5). Within the brain, there are many different functions happening all at once. Being able to determine the location of potential dysfunction is imperative. The main functions of the C4 location in the brain are sensorimotor integration, assistance in

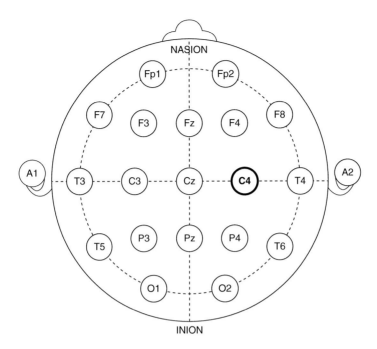

Figure 6.5 Head map graphic highlighting C4 site

calming, left handedness, and short-term memory production (Chapin & Russell-Chapin, 2014). All of these functions are important for healthy brain and optimal functioning. For example, short-term memory is equally important as long-term memory. Short-term memory is essential for processing any new information, which is a key factor for when the brain inevitably comes across previously unencountered information, the storage of multiple tokens of the same type, and variable binding (Norris, 2017). Although brain locations may seem small and insignificant, each section plays a vital role in the brain's functioning.

Implications of Dysregulation

The main cause of dysregulation in C4 is increased levels of beta waves. When a human brain experiences increased levels of beta in C4, the main manifestation is seen as hypervigilance (Chapin & Russell-Chapin, 2014). Hypervigilance is defined by Merriam-Webster (2018) as a "condition of maintaining an abnormal awareness of environmental stimuli." Envision a person who is extremely sensitive to light, sound, or touch. If the stimuli in a certain situation are beyond what the person is comfortable with, this could potentially cause them to lose control and potentially have a panic episode. Of all the functions of C4, sensorimotor integration and inability to self-calm are affected the most by increased levels of beta. Sensorimotor integration is an innate neurobiological process and refers to the "integration and interpretation of sensory stimulation from the environment by the brain to transform such inputs in motor actions" (Machado et al., 2010).

Sensorimotor integration is important for many different functions of life. For example, the ability to comprehend textures and knowing to remove your hand when it comes in contact with a hot surface. When sensorimotor integration is dysregulated, sensory input is not integrated or organized in the proper ways, causing abnormal reactions to certain senses. There are multiple ways this dysregulation can manifest, and also in varying degrees (Machado et al., 2010), including oversensitivity to light and sound, issues with coordination, being unable to tell where the limbs are in space, and issues with engaging in conversation.

Two Neurocounseling Interventions

Sensorimotor integration is most often addressed with an adjunct service of occupational therapy. Within the scope of neurocounseling, it is important to focus on the client's inability to self-calm through the techniques listed below.

Progressive Muscle Relaxation

Step 1: The therapist begins by explaining that Progressive Muscle Relaxation (PMR) is a series of muscle exercises intended to provide full body relaxation. This technique is an assistance tool used to alleviate panic attacks, anxiety, and many other concerns that stem from the inability to self-calm (Ameli, 2014; Center for Clinical Interventions, 2019).

Step 2: The therapist will then begin by telling the client to tighten and contract a specific muscle for 15 seconds and then slowly release the contraction while exhaling.

Step 3: The therapist will then move throughout the whole body, beginning with toes and ascending to the head.

Step 4: After the therapist and client have completed the entire body using PMR, the client will be able to identify the sensory difference between tautness and relaxation.

Step 5: This awareness will allow the client to eventually be able to identify when stress is coming on and being focused in one area. They will then be equipped to use these techniques in their daily lives to identify and attend to the stress and master self-calming.

Length of intervention: 15–20 minutes within a typical session

Mindfulness Meditation (Figure 6.6)

Step 1: The client and therapist should begin this session by identifying trouble areas. In clients who have C4 dysregulation, often issues will present as negative emotions and stress related to sensorimotor regulation.

Step 2: The therapist will then explain that the process of mindfulness meditation involves the client focusing on one object, thought, or sound and returning to this particular thing if the client's mind begins to wander (Mineo, 2018; Wegela, 2010).

Step 3: Once the client decides on where to focus, they will begin to examine the thoughts that enter into their mind while focusing on the object. The client is then instructed to acknowledge these thoughts but let them go, returning their focus to their object of choice.

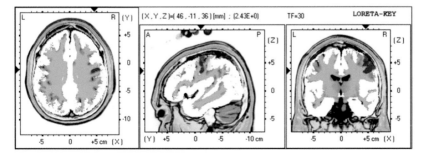

Figure 6.6 LORETA images at C4 during mindfulness meditation

Step 4: Once this method is mastered, the client will be able to use these calming techniques in their day-to-day life when negative thoughts begin to enter their mind. It is important for the therapist to continue to work with the client because one of the main challenges associated with mindfulness meditation is that is takes time and practice and clients should be prepared to train their brain similar to training the body.

Length of intervention: 5–10 minutes within a typical session

Conclusions

Chapter 6 examines the sensory motor cortex, which assists in integrating our sensory motor needs on both sides of the body and coordinating balance and movement. For each of the three sites, C3, CZ, and C4, dysregulation factors and two neurocounseling techniques were presented, as well as LORETA image activations for each site.

References

Ameli, R. (2014). *25 Lessons in Mindfulness: Now time for healthy living*, pp. 90–94. Washington, DC: American Psychological Association.

Berners-Lee, T. & Fischetti, M. (2000). *Weaving the Web: The original design and ultimate destiny of the World Wide Web.* New York: HarperBusiness.

Carter, R. (2014). *The Human Brain Book* (rev. ed.). New York: DK Publishing.

Center for Clinical Interventions (2019). Progressive muscle relaxation. Retrieved from www.cci.health.wa.gov.au/-/media/CCI/Mental-Health-Professionals/Panic/Panic---Information-Sheets/Panic-Information-Sheet---05---Progressive-Muscle-Relaxation.pdf.

Chapin, T.J. & Russell-Chapin, L. (2014). *Neurotherapy and Neurofeedback: Brain-based treatment for psychological and behavioral problems.* New York: Routledge.

Collura, T.F. & Frederick, J.A. (eds.) (2017). *Handbook of Clinical QEEG and Neurotherapy.* New York: Routledge.

Edwards, S. (2015). Dancing and the brain. *On the Brain*, Winter. Retrieved from https://neuro.hms.harvard.edu/harvard-mahoney-neuroscience-institute/brain-newsletter/and-brain-series/dancing-and-brain.

Fissler, P., Küster, O.C., Laptinskaya, D., Loy, L.S., von Anim, C.A.F. & Kolassa, I.T. (2018). Jigsaw puzzling taps multiple cognitive abilities and is a potential protective factor for cognitive aging. *Frontiers in Aging Neuroscience* 10, 299.

Karpati, F.J., Giacosa, C., Foster, N.E.V., Penhune, V.B. & Hyde, K.L. (2016). Sensorimotor integration is enhanced in dancers and musicians. *Experimental Brain Research* 234(3), 893–903.

Machado, S., Cunha, M., Velasques, B., Minc, D., Teixeira, S., Domingues, C.A. & Ribeiro, P. (2010). *Sensorimotor Integration: Basic concepts, abnormalities related to movement disorders and sensorimotor training-induced cortical reorganization.* Retrieved March 19, 2018 from www.ncbi.nlm.nih.gov/pubmed/20859923.

Merriam-Webster (2018). 'Hypervigilance.' Retrieved April 10, 2018 from www.merriam-webster.com/dictionary/hypervigilance.

Mineo, L. (2018). With mindfulness, life's in the moment. *The Harvard Gazette.*

Myers, P. (2011). Why puzzles are good for your child's development. *Child Development Institute.* Retrieved from https://childdevelopmentinfo.com/child-activities/why-puzzles-are-good-for-your-childs-development/#gs.aeq3z1.

Norris, D. (2017). Short-term memory and long-term memory are still different. *Psychological Bulletin* 143(9), 992–1009. DOI:10.1037/bul0000108.

Stuss, D.T. (2011). Functions of the frontal lobes: Relation to executive functions. *Journal of the International Neuropsychological Society* 17(5), 759–765.

Wegela, K. (2010). How to practice mindfulness meditation. Retrieved from www.psychologytoday.com/us/blog/the-courage-be-present/201001/how-practice-mindfulness-meditation.

7

TEMPORAL LOBES (T3, T4, T5, AND T6)

Integrating the World, Myself, and Others

Karoline Pitts, Melissa Hodge, Donna Miller, and Nicole Pacheco

In his fascinating book, *Why Zebras Don't Get Ulcers*, Dr. Robert Sapolsky (2004) believed that "we are uncovering the brain basis of behaviors – normal, abnormal and in-between. We are mapping a neurobiology of what makes us, us." No truer words could be said when understanding the locations and functions of the temporal lobes, T3, T4, T5, and T6.

T3 Location and Function

T3 is located in the left anterior temporal lobe, behind the ear (Figure 7.1). If one were to feel behind their ear, they would feel a bone known as the mastoid process. Directly behind this bone is the T3 area. T3 is associated with its counterpart, T4, which is located in the opposite hemisphere. Regionally, the temporal lobe is typically associated with such processes as language comprehension, sensory input, and memory retention (Brainmaster, 2008). T3, specifically, has several associated functions, including verbal memory formation and storage, phonological processes,

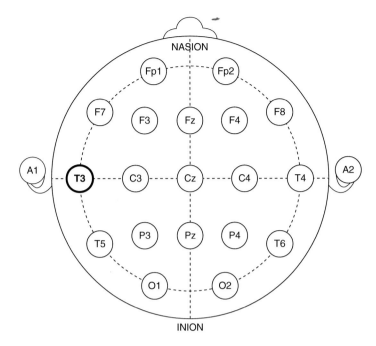

Figure 7.1 Head map graphic highlighting T3 site

hearing, and the ability to remember what you see (Race, Keane & Verfaellie, 2011).

Implications of Dysregulation

People experiencing high concentrations of high beta waves in T3 will present with several symptoms or areas of concern, including memory problems, lack of flexible memory, and trouble processing language (Roohi-Azizi et al., 2017).

People experiencing high concentrations of theta waves may present with concerns such as irritability, stress, and apathy (Roohi-Azizi et al., 2017).

Two Neurocounseling Interventions

The following neurocounseling interventions focus on activating the T3 area. These interventions can be used in a variety of situations, both clinically and personally.

Mnemonic Devices

Mnemonic devices have been shown to accelerate the rate of learning, ease the recall of information, and improve memory (Laing, 2010). They are a useful intervention for an individual struggling with issues related to T3 dysfunction as they incorporate the functions of T3, such as verbal memory formation and language processing. There are four main types of mnemonic devices: acrostics, acronyms, rhyme and song, and visual triggers (Figure 7.2).

Acrostics

Acrostics are utilizing the first letter of each word you are trying to remember and making it into a sentence. For example, a common sentence that piano teachers use to help their students remember their notes is the sentence "All Cows Eat Grass," representing A, C, E, and G notes. This device can be applied in counseling to help individuals with T3 issues remember vital steps to their coping skills.

Acronyms

Acronyms are words composed of the first letters of an idea or phrase you would like to remember. We see examples of this in daily life with companies or agencies which go by abbreviated titles such as NASA, the NSA, or FBI. Acronyms can easily be incorporated into practice by shortening interventions, coping skills, or reminders into short, easy to remember phrases. For instance, when helping individuals with T3 issues who are presenting with concerns such as stress or irritability, the exercise "Just One Breath" or "JOB" is an easy-to-remember skill in which the individual is prompted to focus on one breath, and the feelings that come with it.

Rhyme and Song

Rhyme and song are an easy way to activate the T3 area, as they are involved in the majority of its functions, such as hearing, processing, and comprehension. This technique can be particularly beneficial for children, as they learn to process and explore their emotions and situations they are facing (Vernon, 2009). A simple example is while helping a child work on self-esteem, having them either create or recite a poem, quote, or rhyme about self-acceptance. For instance, "I am amazing, incredible me, celebrate the being I choose to be" (Coppersmith, 2004).

Visual Memory Triggers

Visual triggers are known to improve memory (Rothen, Meier & Ward, 2012). It is simple to incorporate visual triggers into practice. For example, when working with an individual who has difficulty remembering to take medication, they can be prompted to associate their medication with their refrigerator. When they go into their kitchen this visual memory will remind them to take their medications.

Directions

Step 1: Choose the most appropriate mnemonic device for the participant. For example, rhyme and song would typically be used with younger children, while acrostics and acronyms would be used with adults and teenagers.

*This example outlines the use of an acrostic to remember the mindfulness exercise known as "five senses," in which a person mindfully explores their senses in an attempt to ground themselves in the moment.

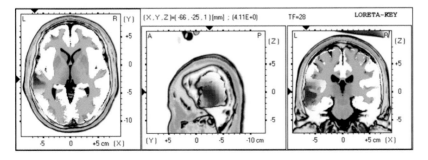

Figure 7.2 LORETA scan during mnemonic intervention

Step 2: Create a sentence, using the first letters of each word, to remember the order of the five senses: hear, smell, see, taste, touch. *A simple acrostic used to remember this exercise could be "Have Some Super Tasty Tacos." The phrase is easy to remember and invokes one of the senses utilized in the exercise.
Length of intervention: 5 minutes

Closed Eye Art

Closed eye art is an art therapy technique that can be applied to help address concerns related to T3. When an individual closes their eyes, they are cutting input from one of the brain's main sources of sensory information. By doing so, blood flow is increased to other areas of the brain, especially those that are still gathering information about our environments. This is commonly referred to as "enhancing other senses" (Brodoehl, Klingner & Witte, 2015). This is especially useful to those with T3 issues, as the T3 point is located behind the ears, and is a main factor in the use of hearing. Additionally, increasing the blood flow to this area has been shown to increase memory (Buchsbaum et al., 2012). Finally, when an individual closes their eyes, it helps to increase concentration and focus (Intuitive Creativity, n.d.). These are all benefits that would be useful to any individual while processing an event or describing a situation. Closed eye art can be applied in a variety of ways. If a client was talking about their family, but having difficulty expressing themselves, or finding the appropriate word to use, a counselor could prompt the individual to close their eyes and draw a picture of their family, stopping at each member to discuss them individually.

Directions

Step 1: Have the participant take a deep breath and close their eyes.
Step 2: Prompt the participant to draw a picture of the subject currently under discussion (i.e., family), while keeping their eyes closed.
Step 3: Have the participant discuss their drawing and the thoughts, feelings, and emotions that they are having while drawing the picture.
Length of intervention: 15 minutes

T4 Location and Function

The T4 site is located by the right ear in the frontal section of the right temporal lobe in the right cerebral cortex (Figure 7.3). T4 is part of the primary auditory cortex, which has neuronal communication with the limbic system to interpret sound input and form and store emotional and autobiographical memory (Carter, 2014). T4 contributes to the development of personality, as well as the ability to hear, recognize patterns, organize, and create music (Chapin & Russell-Chapin, 2014). Thus, T4 helps vary singing and tone, as well as to notice, recall, and interpret melodies, emotionally charged experiences, and the tone and affective quality of voices. It notices when something heard resonates with the listener and if it was spoken in a false or phony way. In other words, T4 weighs the intent implied in the tone of the voice and manages the reaction. Thus, T4 has been suggested to be the Emotive Listener (Nardi, 2016).

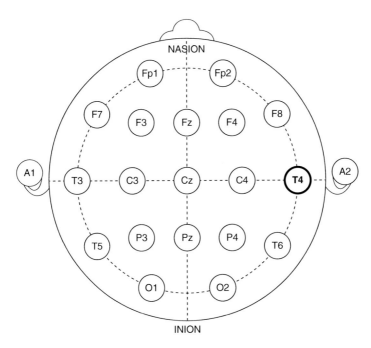

Figure 7.3 Head map graphic highlighting T4 site

Implications of Dysregulation

Implications of dysregulation of the right temporal lobe include distortions in auditory and visual memory, being preoccupied with morals or religion, and experiencing problems with déjà vu, socializing, processing music, determining meaning of verbal tones, and perceiving social cues, facial expressions, and melodies (Chapin & Russell-Chapin, 2014). Specific to T4 include struggles with concentration, tolerance of stress, anger, aggression, sadness, sensitivity to sounds, and interpretation of voice tones. Hostility may be felt if other brain regions do not manage negative sound input before getting to T4 (Nardi, 2009). Moreover, when theta brainwaves that are used to keep the brain calm (Swingle, 2008) and access or discharge memories (Kershaw & Wade, 2011) are greater than 4–7 Hz per minute in T4, it may be more difficult to remain calm, or be creative, reflective, or meditative in response to sound input. This may be seen when a sound or tone of voice is interpreted as negative or threatening, and the sympathetic nervous system is automatically activated like an amygdala highjack (Goleman, 2005). Thus, an irrational quick reaction to fight, flight, or freeze can be initiated instead of a slow rational response to organize, manage, and face the input (Carter, 2014). Such a reaction may involve physical and emotional symptoms. Physical symptoms may include an increase in muscle tension, sweatiness, increased heart rate, tunnel vision, and faster, more shallow breathing. Emotional symptoms could include feeling angry, sad, fearful, disgusted, and surprised (Carter, 2014). Dysfunction of T4 related to excessive or deficient theta brainwaves associates with diagnoses such as attention deficit hyperactivity disorder (ADHD), learning disabilities, post-traumatic stress disorder (PTSD), head trauma (Swingle, 2008), and may explain the phantom sound of tinnitus (Shulman & Goldstein, 2002).

Two Neurocounseling Interventions

Do your Digeridoo

A didgeridoo, one of the world's oldest wind instruments, is used to release emotional stagnation and negative energy. The meditative practice helps heal various physical and mental conditions by connecting the mind and body through unique resonant sounds that activate deep meditative theta and delta brainwave states (Carringer, 2015). Integrate playing a didgeridoo in counseling sessions to promote T4 function.

Step 1: Create or buy a digeridoo (available in travel-size). To promote rapport and creativity, the client can personalize it with quotes or designs while in the session.

Step 2: Practice steady and circular breathing for 10 minutes. It can be practiced with a clear cup of water and a straw. Create a steady flow of bubbles by blowing out through the mouth and simultaneously inhaling through the nose to restore the lungs and cheeks with air. Reassure the client that it takes time to master.

Step 3: Practice playing the digeridoo for 20 minutes. YouTube videos demonstrate how to position the lips, manipulate the mouth and voice box, and use circular breathing to create sounds. Encourage the client to experiment with making sounds that match the environment. The counselor can practice with the client.

Step 4: Identify and process the feelings experienced while and after playing.

Step 5: Have the client practice playing the digeridoo daily for 20 minutes. The client may use it as needed. Suggest playing the digeridoo in nature to mimic environmental sounds.

Step 6: Check in with client at the next session by asking, "Did you play your digeridoo?"

Length of intervention: 30–50 minutes

HumorU

T4 is one region that assists with humor (Nardi, 2009). There are four humor styles, in which self-enhancing and affiliative humor promote adaptation and personal and social well-being (Martin et al., 2003; Schneider, Voracek & Tran, 2018). Integrate HumorU into counseling sessions to promote T4 functioning by building self-enhancing and affiliative humor skills (Figure 7.4).

Step 1: Define the four types of humor: self-enhancing, affiliative, aggressive, and self-defeating. The Humor Styles Questionnaire (Martin et al., 2003) can be used to assess the client's use of humor. Focus on

a. Self-enhancing humor: a coping strategy to bring a humorous and optimistic perspective to stressful situations by laughing at oneself. It promotes internal locus of control and self-compassion that human beings make mistakes. Caution not to engage in self-defeating humor.

   b. Affiliative humor: jokes others may find funny that bring people together. Caution not to engage in aggressive humor that makes fun of others.

Step 2: Ask how able the client is to laugh at themselves or joke with others.

Step 3: Have client identify three examples in the past when they could have laughed at themselves or created a joke for another.

Step 4: Discuss the balance of when to tell a joke or to laugh about something. Emphasize that it takes time to build.

Step 5: Have client practice smiling for 10 seconds. Describe how it helps improve mood.

Step 6: Provide homework. Follow up at the next session. Choose from options below.

   a. Look for humor every day.

   b. Track when laughed at self or joked with someone.

   c. Immerse into humor: attend a comedy or improv workshop, watch humorous videos or shows, be around humorous people.

   d. Create a humorous style using different mediums: words, pictures, objects, parody song.

   e. Think of something that makes you smile.

   f. Practice smiling 10 seconds a day.

     Length of intervention: 30–50 minute

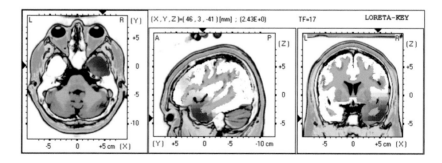

Figure 7.4 LORETA scan of T4 activation after thinking of something that makes you smile intervention

T5 Location and Function

The left and right temporal lobes are found just behind the ears and are the second largest lobes found in the brain, the frontal lobe being the largest (Figure 7.5). ("Brain Map", 2017). The temporal lobes are comprised of the auditory cortex and the hippocampus ("Brain regions", 2016). The auditory cortex controls the processing of information that is heard (auditory) and the hippocampus is involved with memory processes ("Brain regions", 2016). The left temporal lobe is typically dominant to the right in most people and is responsible for understanding language and remembering verbal information ("Brain Map", 2017). The T5 region of the brain is located in the left temporal lobe. The specific function of T5 is to regulate logical and verbal understanding (Bradley University, 2014). This encompasses word recognition, auditory processing, and meaning construction (Bradley University, 2014). This region of the brain also controls short-term memory and inner voice or subconscious thoughts (Bradley University, 2014).

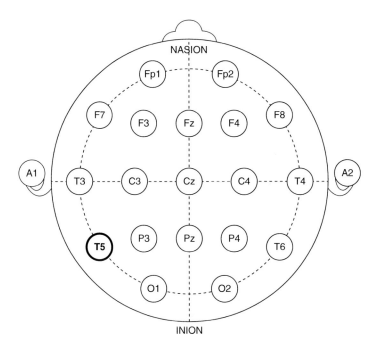

Figure 7.5 Head map graphic highlighting T5 site

Implications of Dysregulation

T5 brain dysregulations in the left temporal lobe cause an increase in theta brainwave activity. This increase can lead to inattention, a decreased understanding of meaning, and spontaneity (Bradley University, 2014). Although theta waves are usually most active during meditative or sleepy states, elevated levels during active times can result in an individual feeling scattered and make someone appear as though they are day-dreaming ("Neurofeedback & Brainwaves", 2016). Theta increases on the left side of the brain are more commonly associated with a lack of organization ("Neurofeedback & Brainwaves", 2016). This dysregualtion can have a negative impact on the ability of the T5 region of the brain to adequately process information and store it in the short-term memory bank, as well as create an inability to regulate one's inner voice when feeling scattered, unorganized, and/or inattentive.

T5 brain dysregulations can also lead to elevated beta brainwaves. According to "Neurofeedback & Brainwaves" (2016), "Beta waves represent our normal waking state of consciousness when attention is directed at cognitive tasks and the outside world". Beta brainwave functioning assists with problem-solving tasks, decision-making processes, and mental activities requiring focused attention ("Neurofeedback & Brainwaves", 2016). An increased level of beta waves can lead to a higher state of confusion, difficulty with reading, and problems with comprehension or finding meaning (Bradley University, 2014). Due to T5 regulating logical and verbal understanding of language processes, this dysregulation can disrupt an individual's ability to recognize words and construct meaning out of these words.

Two Neurocounseling Interventions

Meditative Yoga

One intervention for this dysregualtion is meditative yoga. Meditation used to actively monitor thoughts and feelings in the present moment is an effective treatment for calming the mind and improving focus ("Meditation and Yoga", 2019). By practicing meditative yoga for 20 minutes, twice a week, measured improvements are attained, especially in attention and focus ("Meditation and Yoga", 2019) (Figure 7.6).

Step 1: Select a quiet environment free from noise and distractions with plenty of natural light rather than electric lighting and fresh air flow if possible.

Step 2: Have the client sit on a yoga mat or other soft surface. Start with some light stretching and exercise. In a comfortable seated position on the floor, do a few twists and bends, focusing on the core and back. After stretching, do the following yoga exercises: use two fingers to lightly squeeze the eyebrow several times; roll your eyes in circles several times; rub your temples and jawline; grab your ears and pull downward softly.

Step 3: Do the cat/cow pose. Have the client get on hands and knees. Start with the cat pose by putting your chin down to your chest and slightly arching your back up toward the ceiling while inhaling the breath. Then raise the chin toward the ceiling and dip the spine toward the floor for the cow pose while exhaling. Repeat these poses at least five times each.

Step 4: Practice deep breathing. While still seated in a comfortable position, have the client close their eyes and breathe deeply in through the nose allowing the chest and abdomen to rise. Hold the breath and then exhale completely through the mouth. During this time, have the client think about and embrace the various things that are going on in their life and to embrace the chaos in order to remove exterior distractions and begin to refocus. Continue deep breathing for about five minutes.

Step 5: Ask the client to reflect on their body. With eyes closed and lying on their back in a comfortable position, tense all the muscles for a few seconds then, slowly, from the top of the head to the tips of the toes, instruct the client to release the tension in the body by relaxing all body parts including the jaw, arms, hands, legs, feet, etc.

Step 6: Instruct the client to practice meditative yoga at home at least once a week and continue to conduct yoga during client sessions.
Length of intervention: 20 minutes

Martial Arts

A second intervention for regulating the T5 region of the brain is practicing martial arts. According to Formica (2008), "beyond the physical,

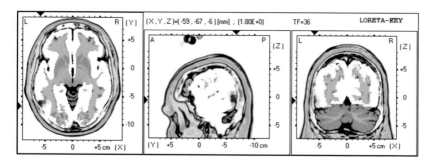

Figure 7.6 LORETA scans from a downward power yoga pose

many of the most valuable lessons of the martial arts are the lessons of social intelligence and mental discipline." Martial arts practices also provide structure, consistency, and ritual in order to assist in the development of "greater organizational and executive functioning skills" (Formica, 2008). If your client is interested and able:

Step 1: Have the client warm up with some simple stretches.

Step 2: Practice punching. With feet planted on the floor, hip width apart, and knees bent, have the client quickly make a punch with their right arm in a forward motion. Repeat with the left arm, doing 10–15 repetitions per arm.

Step 3: Practice kicking. Using a sturdy platform on which to place one foot above the ground, step up on the platform with one leg while kicking forward or sideways with the other leg. If the client is unable to kick, a step up with a knee raise or a simple step up and down will be sufficient. Repeat on each side for 9–12 repetitions.

Step 4: Forearm plank. Starting in a push-up position, making sure the arms are aligned with the shoulders and the head and heels are in a straight line, hold this posture for 20 seconds and concentrate on breathing. Rest and repeat at least 3 times.

Step 5: Chair dips. In a standing position with feet close together, sit down on the edge of a chair. With hands resting palm down on the chair next to the thighs, and elbows bent at a 90-degree angle, straighten arms and lift up from the chair. Lower the rear end down in front of the chair while bending the arms and legs and then, straightening arms, return to the original seated position. Repeat 8–10 times.

Step 6: End with light stretching and relaxation breathing.

Step 7: Instruct the client to practice at least two of the martial arts techniques at least once a week and continue with the exercises during counseling sessions as needed.

Length of intervention: 15 minutes

T10 Location (formerly T6) Location and Function

T10 is located on the right, non-dominant hemisphere in right-handed individuals, along with most left-handed individuals (unless one is a pure left-hand-, left-eye-, and left-foot-dominant person). T10 previously was referred to as T6 and is found laterally between T8 (previously T4) and P8 (formerly P4) (Figure 7.7). According to Thompson & Thompson (2015), the temporal lobe "is a key area in a number of important cognitive functions" (p. 193) and is known for its role in auditory processing as well as short-term and working memory abilities (in the medial aspects). The temporal lobes communicate with the frontal

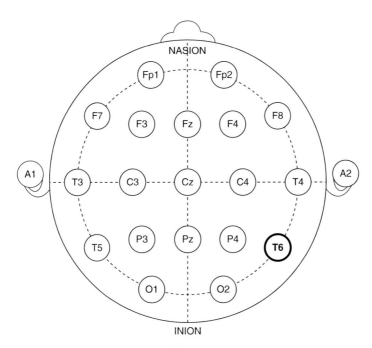

Figure 7.7 Head map graphic highlighting T10 (T6) site

lobes as well as the limbic system and parietal sensory inputs. In addition, the temporal lobes "play a large role in the integration and comprehension of new information and on the emotional valence of thoughts and behaviors" (Thompson & Thompson, 2015, p. 89). In other words, the temporal lobes help us understand new information and label things as either "good" and positive or "bad" and adverse. The more specific functions of T10 include emotional understanding, facial and symbol recognition (along with the fusiform gyrus), auditory processing, and sustained and long-term memory processes (Anderson, 2010).

Implications of Dysregulation

Problems with the right (nondominant) temporal lobe involve tasks of sound and shape perception. Damage to the right temporal lobe can also cause "a loss of inhibition of talking" (Thompson & Thompson, 2015, p. 192) or, in other words, lacking the ability to stop talking. The lack of ability to recognize faces, prosopagnosia, is also found when there is damage to the right temporal lobe. Problems in this area are seen when a person struggles to recognize and remember faces or the melodies of songs. They tend to occur when excess theta waves (4–7 Hz) are present. Thornton (2002) implicated T10, in addition to 23 other areas, with memory ability, especially with immediate and delayed recall. As mentioned above, the temporal lobes work with the fusiform gyrus for sustained attention tasks. The fusiform gyrus plays an important role in helping decrease the sympathetic nervous system response (fight or flight response) by its communication with the central nucleus of the amygdala. Individuals with autism spectrum disorders have been found to have deficient functioning in this area (Thompson & Thompson, 2015).

Two Neurocounseling Interventions

Memory Palace Technique

As mentioned earlier, memory problems can occur when the temporal lobes have been damaged. The Memory Palace technique is a powerful way to remember important information and can be particularly helpful for students (of all ages) as well as a way to help individuals with memory concerns. This technique, or the "Memory Palace," is "a metaphor for any well-known place that you're able to easily visualize" and is so effective because humans are good at "remembering places we know" (Brainpower, 2020). Below are the steps to give to a client to perform this intervention.

Step 1: Choose your "palace"
  a. An ideal palace would be your home or place that you are very familiar with that does not trigger any stressful or traumatic memories. Create a specific path to walk through your home, which helps strengthen the memory creation and retrieval processes. In addition to your home, other possible "palaces" may include an enjoyable walk in a park or area you are familiar with, place of work, school or university, or streets/neighborhoods in your town.

Step 2: Identify specific features to create "memory slots"
  a. Identify specific features or items in each room. If using your home, pick out a particular detail to your front door. Proceed to the next room and identify the next specific detail that you would see. Do this in a methodical and consistent manner, such as left to right. Continue to identify features that you notice as you move in a methodical manner. Each of these features will be used as "memory slots" that you will later use to store information (one piece of information for each feature).

Step 3: Walk through your "palace" listing the features in order (imprinting the palace to memory)
  a. Practice walking through your memory palace until it comes easily. This tends to be naturally easier for visual learners. Brainpower suggests the following for individuals who find this more challenging:
      i.   Walk through your home and verbally identify the specific features.
      ii. Write down the features and practice mentally walking through the house identifying the features out loud.
      iii. Maintain the same point of view with each feature.
      iv. Overlearning is a good thing with this exercise. Practice the walk-through one more time after you believe you have it mastered.

Step 4: Fill the memory slots – combine features with memorization material

    a.   Starting with the front door, associate the material you want to memorize with the front door's feature. For example, the feature of the front door is

    b.   the knocker and you want to remember the groceries you need to pick up at the grocery store. Imagine a cow's head for the knocker. Be as silly and funny as you can, so maybe the cow is mooing hello to you. As you enter the entryway, there's a chicken sitting on her nest of eggs in your umbrella stand (combining umbrella stand with buying eggs). Continue through your palace until all of your groceries have been given a memory slot.

Step 5: Repeating the walk

    a.   Regularly repeating the palace walk further strengthens this exercise. A good strategy is to start from the beginning each time or from time to time (i.e., after two or three new memory slots have been filled). Think of the popular holiday song, "The 12 Days of Christmas," and its effective combination of repetition and memory (even if you don't personally care for the song, you still know what happens on the 5th day).

       Length of intervention: 15–30 minutes (longer initially as creating the memory palace)

Assigning Meaning Technique (T-Chart)

Another function mentioned above that involves T10 is the assigning of positive or negative valence or meaning to things, events, or other individuals. Dweck (2016) has written extensively of the importance of mental flexibility and a "growth mindset." This mindset differs from a "fixed mindset" that is described as rigid, black-and-white/dichotomous thinking, and often is highly stress-producing as one often views success as avoiding failure. The growth mindset, on the other hand, views failure as an important part of the learning process and places less concern on perfectionism or comparing oneself to the performance, abilities, or perceived success of another (Figure 7.8). Ask the client to

Step 1: Recall a recent or past incident that has been relatively stressful. Verbally describe step-by-step the incident.

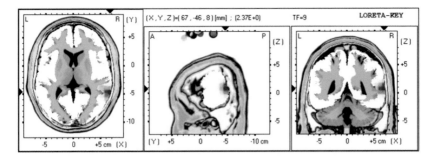

Figure 7.8 LORETA scan of T10 activation during assigning meaning technique (T-Chart) intervention

Step 2: Take a piece of paper and divide it into two columns. Write down both the positive and negative thoughts related to the incident. It is likely that there will be initially more focus on the negative aspects, which is normal and it is important that the individual's experience is normalized and validated.

Step 3: If no positive aspects have been attributed without prompting, encourage the individual to identify at least one important thing the individual has learned from their experience. The counselor may have to provide one example to initiate this process (e.g., the experience illuminated the client's resilience, their ability to trust their intuition, ability to recognize the current pain or hardship has made room for something better, bigger, and more satisfying in the future).

Step 4: Help the client see the importance of exercising mental flexibility and the ability to choose the perception he or she wants to utilize.

Length of intervention: 15–30 minutes

Conclusions

Chapter 7 explores the temporal lobes, which are critical in understanding and interpreting tonality, sounds, and other auditory information, as well as being important integration centers that allow us to incorporate new information with old information. For each of the four sites, T3, T4, T5, and T6, dysregulation factors and two neurocounseling techniques were presented, as well as LORETA image activations for each site.

References

Anderson, J. (2010). Personal Communication. Professional EEG Biofeedback Certification Training. San Rafael, CA: Stens Corporation.

Brainpower (2020). Develop perfect memory with the memory palace technique. Retrieved March 8, 2020 from https://litemind.com/memory-palace.

Bradley University (2014). Physiology and behavior. Retrieved from Bradley University, ENC_607_01_18GJ-.

Brain Map: Temporal lobes (April 18, 2017). Retrieved from www.health.qld.gov.au/abios/asp/btemporal_lobes.

Brain regions, their functions, and neurofeedback (October 26, 2016). Retrieved from http://neurofeedbackalliance.org/brain-regions-and-neurofeedback/.

Brainmaster (February 1, 2008). Positions and brain function. Retrieved from www.brainmaster.com/help/Positions_and_brain_function.htm.

Brodoehl, S., Klingner, C.M. & Witte, O.W. (2015). Eye closure enhances dark night perceptions. *Scientific Reports* 10515. DOI:10.1038/srep10515.

Buchsbaum, B.R., Lemire-Rodger, S., Fang, C. & Abdi, H. (2012). The neural basis of vivid memory is patterned on perception. *Journal of Cognitive Neuroscience* 24(9), 1867–1883.

Carringer, J. (2015). What is didgeridoo sound therapy. *Somatic Psychotherapy Today* 5(4), 78–81. Retrieved from www.somaticpsychotherapytoday.com/wp-content/uploads/2015/09/volume-5-number-4-Fall-2015.pdf.

Carter, R. (2014). *The Human Brain Book*. New York: DK Publishing.

Chapin, T.J. & Russell-Chapin, L. (2014). *Neurotherapy and Neurofeedback: Brain-based treatment for psychological and behavioral problems*. New York: Routledge.

Coppersmith, D. (2004). Hello World. In *The Elusive Here & Now: Inspirational poetry for the soul*. Out of this World.

Dweck, C.S. (2016). *Mindset: The new psychology of success*. New York: Ballantine Books.

Formica, M.J. (July 7, 2008). Martial arts and ADD/ADHD. *Psychology Today*. Retrieved from www.psychologytoday.com/us/blog/enlightened-living/200807/martial-arts-and-addadhd.

Goleman, D. (2005). *Emotional Intelligence: Why it can matter more than IQ*. New York: Bantam Books.

Intuitive Creativity (n.d.). 100 Art Therapy Exercises: The updated and improved list. Retrieved from http://intuitivecreativity.typepad.com/ expressiveartinspirations/100-art-therapy-exercises.html.

Kershaw, C.J. & Wade, J.W. (2011). *Brain Change Therapy*. New York: Norton.

Laing, G.K. (2010). An empirical test of mnemonic devices to improve learning in elementary accounting. *Journal of Education for Business* 85(6), 349–358. DOI:10.1080/08832321003604946.

Martin, R.A., Puhlik-Doris, P., Larsen, G., Gray, J. & Weir, K. (2003). Individual differences in uses of humor and their relation to psychological well-being: Development of the Humor Styles Questionnaire. *Journal of Research in Personality* 37, 48.

Meditation and yoga (2019). Retrieved from www.webmd.com/add-adhd/ adhd-mindfulness-meditation-yoga.

Nardi, D. (2009). *Neuroscience of Personality: Brain savvy insights for all types of people*. West Hollywood, CA: Radiance House.

Nardi, D. (2016). *Neuroscience of Personality: Our brain in colors*. West Hollywood, CA: Radiance House.

Neurofeedback and brainwaves (2016). Retrieved from http:// neurofeedbackalliance.org/understanding-brain-waves/.

Race, E., Keane, M.M., Verfaellie, M. (2011). Medial temporal lobe damage causes deficits in episodic memory and episodic future thinking not attributable to deficits in narrative construction. *Journal of Neuroscience* 31(28), 10262–10269.

Roohi-Azizi, M., Azimi, L., Heysieattalab, S. & Aamidfar, M. (2017). Changes of the brain's bioelectrical activity in cognition, consciousness, and some mental disorders. *Medical Journal of the Islamic Republic of Iran* 31, 53. DOI:10.14196/mjiri.31.53.

Rothen, N., Meier, B. & Ward, J. (2012). Enhanced memory ability: Insights from synaesthesia. *Neuroscience & Biobehavioral Reviews* 36(8), 1952–1963. DOI:10.1016/j.neubiorev.2012.05.004.

Sapolsky, R.M. (2004). *Why Zebras don't get Ulcers*. New York: Holt.

Schneider, M., Voracek, M. & Tran, U.S. (2018). A joke a day keeps the doctor away? Meta-analytical evidence of differential associations of habitual humor styles with mental health. *Scandinavian Journal of Psychology* 59, 289–300. DOI:10.1111/sjop.12432.

Shulman, A. & Goldstein, B. (2002). Quantitative electroencephalography preliminary report-tinnitus. *International Tinnitus Journal* 8(2), 77–86.

Swingle, P.G. (2008). *Biofeedback for the Brain*. New Brunswick, NJ: Rutgers University.

Thompson, M. & Thompson, L. (2015). *The Neurofeedback Book* (2nd ed.). Association of Applied Psychophysiology and Biofeedback.

Thornton, Kirtley E. (2002). Electrophysiological (QEEG) correlates of effective reading: Towards a generator/activation theory of the mind. *Journal of Neurotherapy* 3(6), 37–66.

Vernon, A. (2009). *More what Works when with Children and Adolescents: A handbook of individual counseling techniques*. Champaign, IL: Research Press.

8

PARIETAL LOBES (P3, PZ, AND P4)

Making Sense of One's Experience and the World Around Me

Nicole Pacheco and Maya Ladasky

Author and consultant Dr. Christina Imre (2014) often says that "when you are making sense, and you understand how things work, you become unstoppable." Better comprehension of how the parietal lobes and brain sites, P3, PZ, and P4 work is a first step in making sense of the world around us with sensory perceptions and cognitive inputs.

P3 Location and Function

The P3 site is found in the left hemisphere of the parietal lobe (Figure 8.1). The parietal lobe is posterior of the Rolandic Fissure, which serves as an anatomical separation of the parietal, temporal, and occipital lobes from the frontal lobes. The parietal lobe extends on both hemispheres medially. P3 represents the area between the middle of the parietal lobe (PZ) and the temporal lobe distally. The left hemisphere of the occipital lobe is posterior to P3 (the specific site is O1).

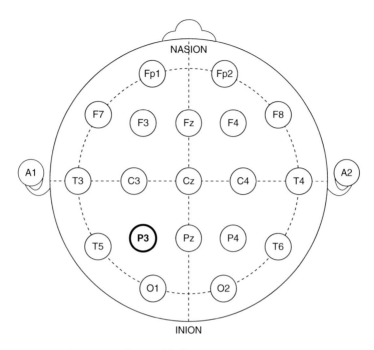

Figure 8.1 Head map graphic highlighting P3 site

The functions of P3 include cognitive processes and sensory perception experienced on the right side of the body. It also plays important roles in the understanding of relationships, multimodal sensations, calculations, movement (praxis), and verbal reasoning.

Implications of Dysregulation

Disruption of normal functioning at P3 is associated with difficulty grasping the meaning or "getting the point" (with excess theta waves, 4–7 Hz), increased confusion, difficult and effortful reading, and/or reading problems, especially identifying key ideas. These latter symptoms tend to occur when excess beta waves (13–35 Hz) are present. Gerstmann syndrome is another sign of left-sided parietal lobe dysfunction. The symptoms of Gerstmann syndrome include "right-left confusion, digital agnosia (inability to name the fingers on both hands), agraphia (inability to write), [and] acalculia (inability to calculate)" (Cozolino, 2017, p. 142).

Amen (2010) observes that obstructive sleep apnea has negative impacts on the parietal lobes. SPECT scans have found decreased left-parietal lobe activity in patients with obstructive sleep apnea. This particular area is required for comprehension, and underperformance can result in "making it difficult to understand conversations or read books" (p. 253). Fortunately, this particular brain impairment can be corrected with continuous positive airway pressure (CPAP) machines.

Two Neurocounseling Interventions

Use of Imagery to Practice Correct Behavior

The psychoneuromuscular theory (or ideomotor principle), originally proposed by British physiologist William Benjamin Carpenter, posits that mentally imagining certain behavior (without physical movement) sends a signal from the brain to the involved muscle or muscle groups. Therefore, especially after an incorrect behavior, it is important to practice imagining the correct behaviors. When a person continues to ruminate on incorrect or wrong behaviors (e.g., accidentally falling in front of people), the brain and body start practice falling again rather than walking smoothly and gracefully. Mentally rehearsing appropriate social behavior can be a helpful way to strengthen this skill and activate several functions of P3 (praxis and multimodal sensations) (Figure 8.2).

Step 1: Have the client position their body in a relaxing, comfortable position.

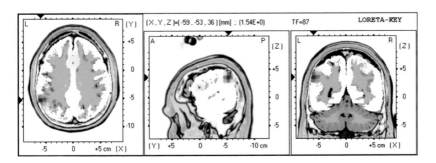

Figure 8.2 LORETA scan of P3 activation during corrective behavior imagery intervention

Step 2: Have the client recall an instant in which they would like to mentally rehearse performing well.

Step 3: Have the client imagine performing the desired behavior. After the client can visualize performing the behaviors smoothly and with ease, have them start to pay attention to other senses to strengthen this behavior. For example, the client can mentally rehearse experiencing the ideal emotions, feelings, or physiological sensations (e.g., relaxed yet alert, feeling as if they are "in the zone"). As appropriate, have the client incorporate other sensory information, such as, sight, smell, and hearing.

Step 4: Gently bring the client's awareness back to the current environment and process his or her experience. If this is the first time this activity has been utilized or a more emotionally intense behavior, the client might report that it was difficult to perform. Normalize and validate this response and remind them of the jagged line of the learning curve.

Step 5: Commend the client for engaging in the activity and identify times and places the client can practice mental rehearsal outside the counselling session.

Length of intervention: 10–20 minutes

5-4-3-2-1 Grounding Activity

Overarousal can induce a stress response, anxiety, anger, and even panic. Underarousal can lead to feelings of lethargy, boredom, and detachment/disengagement. This activity can be used to help individuals practice calming themselves down when they would like to experience a greater sense of calm or engagement. For example, this would be helpful to a person when they notice feelings of anxiety or stress starting. Alternatively, if a person is feeling stuck or unmotivated, this activity can help increase their sense of connection and engagement by disrupting their current cognitive processes and emotional experience.

Step 1: Have the client identify five (5) things in their environment.

Step 2: Have the client identify four (4) sounds in his or her surroundings.

Step 3: Have the client touch three (3) objects.

Step 4: Have the client smell two (2) smells. Help the client identify lotions, lip balm, essential oils, etc., that they can carry with them to also help them reach their desired level of arousal.

Step 5: Have the client notice one (1) gustatory/taste experience. Again, mints, flavored water, tea, etc., can be identified to be utilized by the client.

Length of intervention: 2–5 minutes

PZ Location and Function

The parietal lobes are found towards the back of the brain and are largely responsible for sensory processing and sense of direction (Amen, 2010). PZ is located between the central sulcus (also known as the Rolandic Fissure), the parietal-occipital sulcus, the lateral or Sylvian Fissure, and the medial longitudinal fissure that separates the left and right hemispheres (Figure 8.3). The cuneus and precuneus are two important areas of the parietal lobes. PZ lies in the center of the parietal lobe, between P3 on

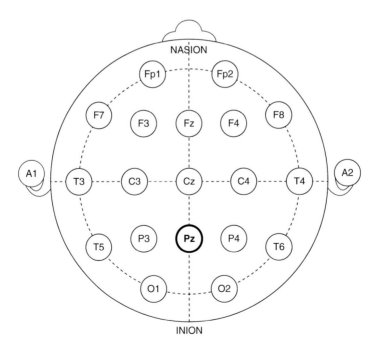

Figure 8.3 Head map graphic highlighting PZ site

the left and P4 on the right. PZ also is the third and last zed or central location if one follows the sites starting at the frontal lobe with FZ, then moving posteriorly to CZ (still in frontal lobe) and finally to PZ in the parietal lobe.

The parietal lobes play important roles in processing visual, emotional, and sensory information. In particular, the parietal lobes have a vital role in the "process[ing] of raw sensory information into perceptions" (Thompson & Thompson, 2015). However, it is the dorsolateral frontal cortex (around the 10–20 site of F7) that decides which information becomes known at a conscious level (Thompson & Thompson, 2015). Both the parietal and occipital lobes play important roles in visual acuity (Thompson & Thompson, 2015). Identification of simple shapes occurs in the occipital lobes whereas more complex pattern recognition takes places in the parietal lobes.

The precuneus and cuneus (both a part of the parietal lobe), along with the posterior cingulate, are areas that are involved in how we view ourselves in relationship to the world. The medial parietal lobe, such as the site of PZ, are particularly important in "self-representation, self-monitoring, and a state of resting consciousness" (Cozolino, 2017, p. 143). Activities about making judgments or self-evaluations in comparison to others, episodic memory retrieval (important and specific memories), and how we view ourselves occur in this area (Thompson & Thompson, 2015). Other functions related to PZ include perception of the midline, spatial relationship, praxis (movement), route finding, and attention shifting/integration.

Implications of Dysregulation

The parietal lobes, along with the insult and anterior cingulate, contribute to one's consciousness. Van der Kolk (2014) found individuals diagnosed with PTSD and severe early-life trauma demonstrated very little activity in the self-sensing part of the brain (including the parietal cortex) on fMRI scans compared to other populations. The parietal lobes are also one of the first areas of the brain that is affected by Alzheimer's Disease (Amen, 2010) and explains "why people with this condition tend to get lost" (p. 23). Amen (2010) also connects the parietal lobes with eating disorders and body-distortion syndromes. In overweight individuals, brain scans have shown that these individuals experience brain loss in the parietal lobes as well as the basal ganglia and corona radiate ("white matter that speeds communication between different parts of the brain," p. 65). In regards to dysregulated brainwave activity at PZ, excess beta (13–35 Hz) has been associated with problems with perseverance and sensory vigilance.

The center image demonstrates activation of PZ, while other areas of the brain are less active, especially on the left temporal and parietal areas and central prefrontal cortex.

Two Neurocounseling Interventions

Route Finding

As discussed above, the parietal lobes are involved in spatial relationship with our environment, movement, and route finding. This intervention incorporates these functions by mentally imagining each step that it takes to go on a route. This intervention may be particularly useful to individuals who feel that their sense of direction is deteriorating or who are showing signs of dementia.

Step 1: Select a starting point (point A) and desired destination (point B).
Step 2: Have the client mentally (and verbally, if desired) break down each important step, turn, or movement to go from point A (original place) to point B (destination).
Step 3: Have the client observe additional information or details of this experience (e.g., make the right turn at the gas station with the large flag; go past the park with the tennis courts) to further cement this route in the client's mind.
Step 4: Repeat the exercise until the client feels that he or she can successfully go from point A to point B.
Length of intervention: 1–5 minutes

Correcting Maladaptive Early Recollections

Utilizing early memories or recollections in psychotherapy was a technique to understand a client's "pattern of life" that began with the early twentieth-century psychoanalyst Alfred Adler (Ansbacher & Ansbacher, 1956). A part of current Adlerian training includes the collection of approximately half a dozen early memories, recalled in present time as a part of the initial stages of psychotherapy. Early recollections can be used as a way to understand a person's view of him or herself, others, and what he or she must do in order to have a place in the world. Ansbacher & Ansbacher (1956) provide these three important considerations when thinking about early recollections: "(a) A recollection is an action of the individual, rather than being 'caused' by a particular experience; he 'chose' to retain this particular incident. (b) The recollection is to an unknown degree at variance from objective facts and to this extent the individual's own construction. (c) Within a given recollection, how the individual responded to the situation is more important than the situation itself" (p. 135).

Maladaptive early recollections can be changed, edited, and modified to help a client move in a more helpful, positive, and possibly empowered way, depending upon his or her goals. For example, an anxious client who is so afraid or fearful about making a mistake that he or she becomes paralyzed at times may recall an early memory involving being scolded by a caregiver after accidentally knocking over a glass of milk. The client can edit the memory to where the caregiver responds in a loving and non-critical manner and supports the client by helping clean up the milk or providing clean clothes (Figure 8.4).

Step 1: Have the client recall an early memory and state it in the present tense as if it were occurring right now.

Step 2: Ask the client to identify the part of the memory that is most vivid. Then ask them why this part is most vivid.

Step 3: Ask the client to identify all the emotions and feelings they experienced in the memory. Again, follow up each emotion by gently asking "why" to further understand their personal construction and beliefs.

Step 4: Note and discuss the presence or absence of others in the memory. Were they helpful or unhelpful?

Step 5: Note and discuss the locus of control in the memory. Was the client able to take care of themselves or were they reliant upon others? Was the client effective in their ability to reach their goals or desired outcome?

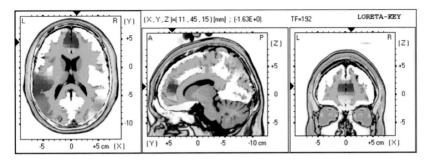

Figure 8.4 LORETA image of PZ during correcting early memory intervention

Step 6: After fully exploring the nature of the early recollection, ask
the client to engage in a moment of introspection to see areas in
their life where similar emotions, interpersonal themes, or events
may be present.
Length of intervention: 40–50 minutes

P4 Location and Function

The P4 region lies in the right hemisphere of the brain and is part of
the parietal lobe (Figure 8.5; Anderson, 2010). The parietal lobe, located
between the frontal and occipital lobes, is separated into two functional
areas, one for sensation and perception and one for incorporating that
sensory input (Kandel, Schwartz & Jessell, 1991). Accordingly, the parietal lobe is responsible for many functions including processing raw
sensory information, perceiving one's own physical body, and taking
part in motor functions including touch, pressure, temperature, taste,
pain, spatial relations, and navigation (Chapin & Russell-Chapin, 2014).
Anderson (2010) notes that major functions of the P4 area include left-
side perception and cognitive processing, spatial relations, multimodal
interactions, praxis, non-verbal resonating, visual-spatial sketchpad, vigilance, and victim mentality.

Implications of Dysregulation

When the parietal lobe is suffering from dysregulation, problems may
occur involving attention, information processing, inability to understand

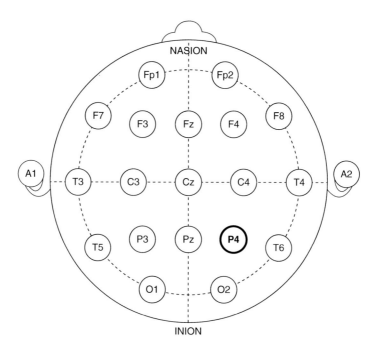

Figure 8.5 Head map graphic highlighting P4 site

spatial relations, and hypervigilance. More specifically, dysregulation in the P4 region of the brain can occur in the form of overactive theta waves and overactive beta waves. High theta waves may prompt intense amounts of self-concern and over-rationalization, whereas high beta waves may prompt extreme emotional rumination (Chapin & Russell-Chapin, 2014).

Increased theta waves may cause an individual to have a heightened sense of self-concern or hypervigilance, which is being on edge and overly concerned about interactions with the environment and with other people. This sense of self-concern could also present as anxiety-related symptoms. As described previously, P4 is associated with a victim mentality. Victim mentality may increase with dysregulation in this area, much like self-concern. People with this dysregulation may embody a notion that the world is out to get them, they may be concerned about their interactions with others, and cognitively put themselves into a perceived position of being taken advantage of or judged by others. Over rationalization, which is also characteristic of dysregulation in this area, is closely related to self-concern. These individuals may bestow unrealistic or overly generalized causes for their actions or actions of others. This could increase victim mentality and could lead the person to place concerns and causes on situations that are not based in reality.

Overactive beta waves can result in emotional rumination, which can be simply defined as dwelling on negative feelings. These negative feelings could stem from any variety of situations including, for example, a boss's reprimand for a mistake at work or an argument with a loved one. The emotional rumination comes after the event, when the individual who experienced it is left thinking constantly about what they could have done differently to alleviate the problem. Although reframing old problems to come up with new solutions can certainly be beneficial, spending too much time on it can keep a person from functioning normally in everyday life. So what are some ways to stop the cycle of emotional rumination? Each client will respond differently to different interventions, but as Selby (2010) notes, one must "engage in some kind of activity that fully occupies your mind and prevents your thoughts from drifting back to the problem." It is important to find an activity that is specific to each client and that each client enjoys, but two general categories of intervention that could decrease emotional rumination are brain-teasing activities and freestyle art.

Two Neurocounseling Interventions

Brainteasers

The goal of the brainteaser intervention is to stimulate the left hemisphere of the brain, which is concerned with logic and reasoning (Carter, 2019). Possible worksheets to do with the client include word searches, crossword or sudoku puzzles, or trivia quizzes. The activity should be tailor-made to a client's interests. For instance, a sports-based trivia quiz could be created for an athletic client or a word search on plants could be used for a client interested in gardening. Importantly, the achievement and accuracy of answers in the activity are not as important as the way the client responds to it. The goal is to take a step back from the emotional rumination; the client is not avoiding the problem but is instead detaching from it temporarily and then coming back with a fresh perspective (Selby, 2010).

Step 1: Ask the client to rate their mood on a scale of 1 to 5, with 1 being the lowest.

Step 2: Have the client select a worksheet on a topic of their interest.

Step 3: Set a timer for 15 minutes in which both the counselor and client perform the activity.

Step 4: Go over the results.

Step 5: Solicit feedback on the activity and again ask for a rating of mood on a scale of 1 to 5.

Length of intervention: 25 minutes

Sandplay Therapy

The goal of sandplay therapy is to increase regulation in the P4 area by providing a bilateral experiential therapeutic technique that helps clients conceptualize their social interactions. In addition, it provides the opportunity to reframe negative interactions and related cognitions into a more realistic and positive perspective. Sandplay therapy is a psychotherapeutic technique that utilizes miniature figurines arranged by a client in a small sandbox in order to represent dimensions of the client's social reality (Jones-Smith, 2016).

This sort of play involves many of the stimulating aspects of the P4 region such as using the left side of the body through manipulating figurines with both hands. It involves spatial relations by the proximity of figurines in the sandbox or stage area and then changing the spatial relations between these figurines. This approach involves seeing, hearing, and feeling the therapeutic process, which achieves the multimodal process. Praxis could be utilized by having a client act out a negative situation or event by using the figurines in the sandbox and then reflecting upon it in a safe manner (Figure 8.6).

Step 1: Invite the client to utilize sandplay figurines in a sandbox or stage-like area to create a scene of a recent social interaction that left them feeling upset.

Step 2: Ask the client to describe the scene they created, to narrate the conversation that occurred, and to describe their thoughts and feelings related to the interaction.

Step 3: The counselor prompts the client to gain more realistic understandings of their social interactions through questions

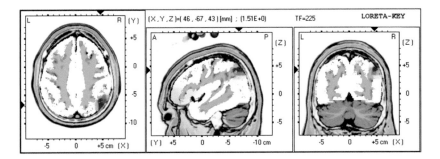

Figure 8.6 LORETA scan of P4 activation after sandplay intervention

   aimed to shed light on potential areas of over-rationalization and self-concern that may not be warranted.

Step 4: The counselor helps the client to generalize the content that the client expresses in step three to their social interactions.

Step 5: The counselor invites the client to change the interaction by re-narrating it with their newfound ideas, perhaps even just by asking the client to describe how their thoughts and feelings could be different and more beneficial to the situation.

Step 6: The counselor aids the client in coming up with strategies for applying newfound rational thought processes to future social situations.

Length of intervention: 45 minutes

Conclusions

Chapter 8 explores the parietal lobes, which play an important role in the areas of visual acuity and pattern recognition. They also help us make sense of raw sensory material and turn this information into useful perceptions. For each of the three sites, P3, PZ, and P4, dysregulation factors and two neurocounseling techniques were presented, as well as LORETA image activations for each site.

References

Amen, D.G. (2010). *Change your Brain Change your Body*. New York: Random House.

Anderson, J. (2010). Personal Communication. Professional EEG Biofeedback Certification Training. San Rafael, CA: Stens Corporation.

Ansbacher, H.L. & Ansbacher, R.R. (1956). *The Individual Psychology of Alfred Adler: A systematic presentation in selections from his writings.* New York: Basic Books.

Carter, R. (2019). *The Human Brain Book* (2nd ed). New York: DK Publishing.

Chapin, T.J. & Russell-Chapin, L. (2014). *Neurotherapy and Neurofeedback: Brain-based treatment for psychological and behavioral problems.* New York: Routledge.

Cozolino, L.J. (2017). *The Neuroscience of Psychotherapy* (3rd ed.). New York: W.W. Norton & Company.

Imre, C. (2014). *The Hidden Language of the Mind Self-Help Guide: Explaining the hard stuff the easy way.* Kindle edition.

Kandel, J., Schwartz, J. & Jessell, T. (1991). *Principles of Neural Science* (3rd ed). New York: Elsevier.

Jones-Smith, E. (2016). *Counseling and Psychotherapy: An integrative approach* (2nd ed). Thousand Oaks, CA: SAGE.

Selby, E.A. (2010). *Rumination: Problem solving gone wrong. How rehashing the situation can ruin your mood.* Retrieved from www.psychologytoday.com/us/blog/overcoming-self-sabotage/201002/rumination-problem-solving-gone-wrong.

Thompson, M. & Thompson, L. (2015). *The Neurofeedback Book* (2nd ed.). Wheat Ridge, CO: Association of Applied Psychophysiology and Biofeedback.

Van der Kolk, B.A. (2014). *The Body Keeps Score.* New York: Penguin Books.

9

OCCIPITAL LOBES (O1 AND O2)

Visualizing the World through Recognition and Patterns

Parneet Sahota

Coach and writer Chgyam Trungpa believes that "becoming awake involves seeing our confusion more clearly." Since the occipital lobes are responsible for the majority of our visual processing and patterning, giving ourselves time to figure out and interpret what we see is essential to daily living. Allowing confusion to enter into the picture and learning to be comfortable with the uncomfortable eases some anxiety about all that is surrounding us. The location and functions of both O1 and O2 will be discussed in this chapter.

O1 and O2 Location and Function

The human brain is separated into four lobes and these lobes work in conjunction with one another for smooth and efficient functioning. The right and left occipital lobes each have distinct visual functions, though they interact seamlessly with each other making various visual functions possible. The occipital lobes are the most rear or posterior lobe of the forebrain (Carter, 2014). The occipital lobes comprise Brodmann area 17, the primary visual cortex, and Brodmann areas 18 and 19, the visual processing areas in the secondary visual cortex (Figure 9.1).

The functions associated with O1 and O2 include the processing of information associated with vision, visual acuities, operational and measurable memories, and dreams. The visual consciousness of depth and edge, as well as perception about things, places, and people, is essential in day-to-day navigation, safety, and security of the person and their dependents. In addition, the areas of O1 and O2, in conjunction with other brain regions, hold responsibility in the tasks of reading, writing, spelling, comprehension of reading and writing, drawing, identification of objects, and recognition of places and their associations to self.

Implications of Dysregulation

Damage or deterioration of the occipital lobes can lead to issues with reading, writing, perception, visual memory, etc. Visual information concerning meanings is assimilated in the secondary visual cortex and damage or injury can cause visual agnosia. Visual agnosia can lead to issues recalling words, names, or identity or meaning of a function upon seeing a visual stimulant, and is associated with low-amplitude brainwaves.

A study conducted by Dadashi et al. (2015) found clients diagnosed with generalized anxiety disorder (GAD) demonstrated low amplitude of the alpha and theta brainwaves in the O1 and O2 area of the occipital lobes compared to subjects without the diagnosis of GAD. The researchers were able to see successful reduction of the symptoms when neurofeedback was used to increase the amplitude of theta and alpha waves (Dadashi et al., 2015). Chao, Lenoci & Neylan (2012) observed a relationship between the severity in post-traumatic stress disorder (PTSD) symptoms and reduced gray matter volume in the left occipital lobe, as well as reduced functional ability (Chao, Lenoci & Neylan, 2012). In addition, Swingle (2008) observed that the effects of emotional trauma can be seen at O1 and CZ with low alpha wave amplitude.

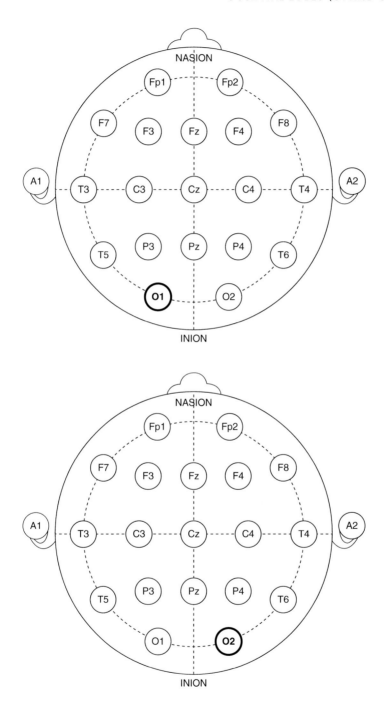

Figure 9.1 Head map graphic highlighting O1 and O2 sites

Neurocounseling Interventions

Audio-Visual Entrainment (AVE)

Audio-visual entrainment (AVE) is efficiently used in the treatment of a number of psychological and medical disorders, including post-traumatic stress disorder (PTSD), attention deficit disorder (ADD), chronic pain, and seasonal affective disorder (SAD) (Siever, 2014). AVE uses sounds and pulses of light at various frequencies to steer the brainwaves into specific patterns. Xenon strobe light and LEDs, along with harmonic content, are used in a rapid on-and-off simulation causing the entrainment, or guiding the brainwave activity in the desired direction.

The practical use of this technique can enhance the relaxation level, positively affect the mood, improve sleep performance, and fine-tune one's cognitive mind (Audio-Visual Entrainment (AVE), 2018). The entrainment generates a state of deep relaxation and can be augmented with the use of diaphragmatic breathing and other relaxation strategies (Siever, 2014) (Figure 9.2).

Individuals who suffer from light-induced seizures and migraine headaches should not use AVE devices.

Step 1: Have the client find a comfortable position.

Step 2: Place headphones on the client's head, making sure that the left headphone covers the left ear and the right headphone covers the right ear. This is particularly important as some programs targeting depression symptoms help to correct brainwave asymmetries by stimulating each ear differently.

Step 3: Place eyeglasses on the client's face. The light does not hurt if the client has their eyes open during the entrainment, but most will find it more relaxing with eyes closed.

Step 4: Start the desired AVE program on the AVE device. Some programs are designed to promote focus and concentration, while others are concerned with relaxation. AVE programs that stimulate faster brainwave activity should not be utilized in the evening to avoid disrupting the natural circadian rhythm cycle.

Step 5: Observe the client and provide them with a glass of water after the exercise. It is important to have the client rise slowly, especially if they were in a reclined position during the entrainment

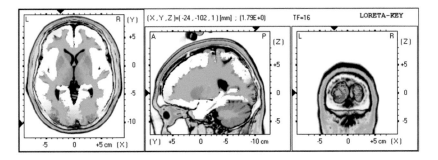

Figure 9.2 LORETA scan of O1 activation during AVE intervention

program, to avoid orthostatic hypertension. Take a moment to discuss the client's experience during the entrainment exercise as well as pre- and post-AVE activity.

Length of intervention: Approximately 15 minutes to 45 minutes or longer (depending on program selected)

Light Therapy Box

Light therapy has been used to effectively treat post-traumatic stress disorder (PTSD), assist with mood regulation, and treat seasonal affective disorder (SAD), as well as improve sleep hygiene and cognitive performance (Seasonal Affective Disorder Information, 2018). Light boxes, lume lamps, and light visors are used as natural techniques to improve mood and productivity in people (Seasonal Affective Disorder (SAD) Information, 2018). The use of a light box can adjust the circadian rhythm, directly affecting a person's sleep cycle and hormonal regulation.

The light is transmitted to the brain and triggers the production of serotonin. If used for seasonal affective disorder a person should use it within the first half hour of waking up (Seasonal Affective Disorder Information, 2018). A person can also customize the light box according to their need, effectiveness, and tolerance by selecting the intensity of the lux light. Full spectrum or white cool fluorescent lights can be used according to a person's preference (Seasonal Affective Disorder (SAD) Information, 2018).

The therapy should be conducted in consultation with a professional and a medical doctor; it may not be recommended for people with bipolar disorder (Seasonal Affective Disorder (SAD) Information, 2018).

Step 1: Person sits in the direct light or at an angle to a full-spectrum light for a set amount of time.

Step 2: Establish an efficient sleep and light therapy schedule that fits the client's personal preference. As mentioned above, using light therapy within 30 minutes of wakening is recommended for individuals suffering from SAD.

Step 3: Adjust and make any necessary changes to the individual's sleep and light therapy accordingly over time.

Length of intervention: Varies from 20 min to 2 hours

Conclusions

Chapter 9 reviews the location and function of the occipital lobes, O1 and O2. Located at the rear of the head directly connected with the optic nerves, the functions associated with O1 and O2 include the processing of information associated with vision, visual acuities, operational and measurable memories, dreams and visual patterning, edge perception, and much of daily living. Dysregulation was discussed along with two neurocounseling interventions.

References

Audio-Visual Entrainment (AVE) (2018). Retrieved from https://mindalive.com/index.cfm/technology/ave/.

Carter, R. (2014). *The Human Brain Book*. New York: DK Publishing.

Chao, L., Lenoci, M. & Neylan, T. (2012). Effects of post-traumatic stress disorder on occipital lobe function and structure. *Neuroreport* 23(7), 412–419.

Dadashi, M., Birashk, B., Taremian, F., Asgarnejad, A.A. & Momtazi, S. (2015). Effects of increase in amplitude of occipital alpha & theta brain waves on global functioning level of patients with GAD. *Basic Clinicial Neuroscience* 6(1), 14–20.

Seasonal Affective Disorder (SAD) Information (2018). Retrieved from http://sad.psychiatry.ubc.ca/resources/public-resources/light-therapy-procedure-for-using-the-10000-lux-fluorescent-light-box/.

Siever, D. (2014). *Audio-Visual Entrainment: Finding a Treatment for Post-Traumatic Stress Disorder*. Alberta: Mind Alive.

Swingle, P.G. (2008). *Biofeedback for the Brain: How neurotherapy effectively treats depression, ADHD, autism, and more*. New Brunswick, NJ: Rutgers University Press.

10

COMING FULL CIRCLE

Lori Russell-Chapin, Nicole Pacheco, and Jason DeFord

This final chapter will summarize and connect all aspects from Chapters 1–9 into a solidifying neurocounseling plan of action. In addition, each co-editor will share what discoveries were learned along the way in writing this book. Author and writer Richard Broadwell reiterates beautifully the purpose of this book:

> We sit on the threshold of important new advances in neuroscience that will yield increased understanding of how the brain functions and of more effective treatments to heal brain disorders and brain diseases. How the brain behaves in health and disease may well be the most important question of our lifetime.
>
> (Broadwell, 1995)

In Section 1, the chapter authors offered the history behind neurocounseling and needed key definitions. Strategies for a comprehensive evaluation and treatment plans were delineated in order to customize goals and protocols for every client. The case of Patrice demonstrated how these neurocounseling constructs, assessments, and interventions could be integrated into everyday talk therapy sessions.

Section 2 emphasized applied science and practical skills using the 19 different locations of the brain from the International 10–20 System. In every chapter the Head Map of Functions diagram displayed each selected brain site, function, consequences of dysregulation, and possible talk therapy interventions for that location. A corresponding LORETA brain scan depicted targeted brain activation during one of those corresponding neurocounseling interventions.

A definition of neurocounseling is "the integration of neuroscience into the practice of counseling by teaching and illustrating the physiological underpinnings of many of our mental health concerns" (Russell-Chapin, 2016, p. 93). As a reader of this text, you have seen this definition practically applied over and over again with each of the brain locations, functions, and areas of dysregulation. Teaching others the value of "bridging our brain to behaviors" reinforces the bi-directionality of our system. The brain communicates to the body, and the body certainly talks to the brain. Sometimes the phrase "top-down and bottom-up or bi-directionality" is also used (Strack, Linden & Wilson, 2011). Clients begin to understand how not caring for one aspect of our brain or body impacts and interacts with the rest of our system. Brain health begins to enter the life of clients.

Talk therapy does help the majority of clients, but for some clients it is just not enough. "We need to better understand the biological basis of behavior and learn how to harness its potential for our clients' benefit" (Russell-Chapin & Chapin, 2020, p. 305). By better understanding the biological basis of behavior, whether that be through a quantitative EEG watching recorded brainwaves or observing a certain demonstrated behavior, these often measurable clues and data assist with a more uniquely personalized treatment.

The four neurocounseling steps to comprehensive treatment planning were presented in Chapter 3 by Ted Chapin, in which neurocounseling is differentiated, somewhat, from talk therapy. These four steps are prioritizing the presenting problems, determining the brain locations that are implicated and targeted from the neurological assessment, selecting an appropriate neurocounseling intervention, and identifying behavioral goals to increase the client's neuroplasticity and reduction of symptoms. Again, this does not replace conventional talk therapy.

Here are major reasons and benefits for integrating neurocounseling interventions into your clinical work. Many of these have been adapted from a previous article by Russell-Chapin (2016) and Field, Jones & Russell-Chapin (2017). The following ideas may assist you in remembering these neurocounseling benefits:

- Neurocounseling teaches clinicians and clients how and why counseling changes the brain.
- Using brain-based approaches may help in better understanding the unique needs of every client.
- Teaching clients and offering psychoeducational materials may assist in understanding the whys and hows of certain symptoms and behaviors.
- Neurocounseling reminds all of us of the mind-body connection and use of integrated resources.
- Computer-assisted technology such as biofeedback, neurofeedback, and other assessments not only examines the source of the dysregulation but can train that dysregulated part of the brain to become functioning and regulated.
- Neurocounseling works with chronic problems, but it is also helpful with peak and optimal performance.
- Neurocounseling teaches clients intrinsic locus of control and personal accountability through practicing emotional, behavioral, and physiological self-regulation and safety.
- Neurocounseling offers added value to all of the counseling professions by expanding the array of available treatments.
- Practicing neurocounseling and brain-based approaches provides more opportunities to create a group of professionals that can become a part of your treatment team, whether that is a pharmacist, nutritionist, neurofeedback specialist, or psychiatrist.
- Neurocounseling emphasizes the need for quantitative outcome measures for treatment effectiveness.
- Neurocounseling techniques must adhere to all counseling ethical guidelines for counselor competency and efficacy and client protection.
- Neurocounseling interventions need supervision to ethically implement safe and sound practices.
- Neurocounseling offers additional evidenced-based research to support its teaching and tenets.

These benefits may be re-emphasized in the following few pages as each of the co-editors shares what they have gained from the inception of this text to its completion. There seem to be similar yet different discoveries.

LORI: I continue to teach graduate students and clients about neurocounseling and the connection between the brain and body. I say this to every student and client. This is a quote from another neurocounseling book:

> As Lori likes to say, once you have learned about how the brain works in relationship to physical and emotional health, you cannot go back. We are confident that this knowledge will forever change how you approach case conceptualization, assessment and intervention in clinical practice.
>
> (Field, Jones & Russell-Chapin, 2017, p. xiii)

I will take those statements even farther now. Neurocounseling may change how we all live our lives as well! Taking charge of our own brain and body gives us more internal locus of control. Once many of my clients learn neurocounseling techniques, they often make similar comments. I will never forget the client who literally skipped out of my office when she was able to control her own peripheral skin temperature. She exclaimed, "If I can control my skin temperature, I wonder what else I can control?" Integrating neurocounseling into our talk therapy sessions offers clients even more accountability for their lives.

Last summer my husband, Ted, and I traveled to Marquette University to take a course titled Neuroanatomical Dissection: Human Brain and Spinal Cord. There we learned about the intricacies of the brain, but actually holding and dissecting a human brain was the most remarkable experience! First, I was very touched by the men and women who gave their brains to science after death. Every person in our class learned so much from their gifts. I have so much more appreciation for the human brain. For me finally dissecting the brain enough to locate the amygdala was the biggest treasure. I was able to hold in my hand this tiny part of the brain that is often responsible for so much in our lives. I marvel at this three-pound organ and all of its incredible networks and functions. We also looked at many diseased brains from alcoholism to strokes.

We discussed at length whether knowing and seeing more about this masterful organ would help us all want to take better care of our brain and bodies!

That being said, what I have learned specifically from co-editing and writing this book is that the brain does not function in isolation. We have presented these neurocounseling skills and shown location activation for certain interventions. However, the brain and body are constantly seeking self-regulation and allostasis. When healthy, the brain and body work together beautifully. When the brain is able to communicate well with other brain locations, an incredible symphony occurs. Sometimes in this musical event called life, the flute section needs to be dominant, but the other sections remain alert and ready to participate when called to action. When all instruments are well-tuned and play for the finale, the product is beautiful and harmonic. The same holds true for our brain: when it is regulated and communicating with all brain lobes, a person functions and feels well socially, physically, emotionally, behaviorally, spiritually, and occupationally. When this occurs, the brain is able to use the right brainwaves for the right task at the right time (Chapin & Russell-Chapin, 2014).

In addition, I have learned that neurocounseling interventions need to be intentional, I suppose like every other counseling skill. Choosing a specific technique for a particular brain area can build stronger neuronal pathways. Remember the Hebbs Rule, "Neurons that fire together, wire together" (Hebbs, 1949). These intentional neurocounseling skills assist our clients in building stronger and more reinforced brain connections for healthier positive plasticity.

Locating the dysregulated areas of your client's brain can be seen behaviorally, as we have discussed in a handshake and voice intonation, but for those chronic brain concerns, utilizing known quantifying outcomes such as EEGs and other standardized instruments can assist counselors in creating customized treatment plans. Locate trusted clinicians in your area, and refer to them. Strengthen your clinical team for even stronger outcomes and client success.

NICOLE: In our training to become mental health providers, we are taught the importance of meeting our clients where they are. My training was at the Adler School of Professional Psychology, where the famous Alfred Adler quote was repeated: we must "walk in our client's shoes."

That is, we must understand their perception of themselves, others, and the world and honor their life experiences with an open mind and empathetic heart. I believe neurocounseling is another valuable vehicle of providing insight, awareness, and validation to clients and providers.

Therapeutic relationships and alliances are built on trust. How exciting would it be to work with a provider who not just understands my experiences, but can educate me about why my brain is doing what it is doing, and more importantly, help me build an effective brain toolbox that I can implement outside the session? As a provider, the validation I see clients experience when we talk about neurocounseling and neuromodulation (i.e., what is going on with the brain and let's start doing things to help it be more efficient or regulated) is outstanding and highly rewarding. We may not like the symptoms of a dysregulated brain, but that powerful knowledge of what is happening in our brain and that there are things within my own volition to improve my brain provides us with a wonderful opportunity to start the healing process with validation and acknowledgement.

Our work with neurocounseling extends beyond the client. This is frequently seen when working with children, as parents and caregivers are often observing, or ideally, practicing self-regulation skills themselves. We are able to educate families about brain health and support them in making healthy life-style choices, understand and handle difficult emotions with more ease, and live healthier, happier lives. How wonderful would it be where previously coined "disruptive" or "pathological" behavior was viewed as less than ideal brainwave activity (e.g., dysregulated theta in the frontal regions) that could be positively affected by engaging in diaphragmatic breathing for a few minutes?

Neurocounseling extends beyond the elimination of negative symptoms. A client I have worked with for several years originally started to see me to improve her tennis game. During our work together, she suffered an injury that forced her to quit tennis and find a new sport. She quickly picked up her new sport (golf) and, along with the guidance of a golf pro, has excelled at her new sport and has received a number of awards and accolades. She implements a number of neuromodulation skills and metacognitive skills to improve her physical and mental game (also called psychophysiological performance) and overall well-being. She has overcome challenges, learned new ways of dealing with difficult circumstances and people, and is enjoying her health, hobbies, and activities. She recently shared that the most important thing she has gained through our work together is that she has learned what joy is and how to live a joyful life. What a truly lovely and amazing gift to give to oneself!

As we continue to learn more about the brain, we also realize there is so much more that we do not know (for example, we still don't know what part of the brain generates alpha brainwave activity). We know that the brain is highly plastic and resilient. At a fundamental level, I view neurocounseling as an effective mechanism to provide us with the opportunity to realize the power of choice, the importance of self-growth and learning, and that the journey towards health (and joy) begins with understanding, acceptance, and a gentle, nurturing response. This builds on the work that mental health providers are already accomplishing. With neurocounseling and neuromodulation skills, we are expanding and strengthening our therapeutic effectiveness. We're helping clients see that

> By understanding how my brain is operating, I understand and accept why I might be having these thoughts or experiencing these emotions. Therefore, I will respond with appreciation of the current circumstance and in a manner that will be beneficial and lead me in the direction I seek.

JASON: I think what sticks out to me the most, and was illustrated earlier in the book, is that the mental health profession is the only profession that doesn't actually look at what we are treating: the brain. This is why the role of neurocounseling becomes so important to us and our clients. Even though we may not have access to EEG equipment or brain scanning technologies, we can have a good idea of what is happening in our clients' brains by understanding basic neurophysiology and brain activity alongside self-assessments that are more directed at brain health. As we gather this information, we are better able to give directed and practical advice and interventions to our clients as a way to be more efficient in treating them.

One thing that I consistently hear clients say is that they feel validated in their experience of struggles and symptoms. We are able to educate, and potentially show them, that brain dysregulation is causing these symptoms, but also that we can help them self-regulate and lessen or eliminate these very same symptoms. When this shift from feeling controlled by their diagnosis to being in control of regulation and brain health happens, they are more motivated to make positive changes and see that there is "light at the end of the tunnel." With more of an internal motivation and locus of control, outcomes often come more frequently and quicker than traditional counseling.

As this book has highlighted, there are many different types of neurocounseling interventions, many of which can be helpful for different areas of the brain. Rather than being stuck in one type of theoretical orientation, we are able to use creative ways to challenge our clients and make therapy "fun" for them in doing so. Once the brain is better regulated and our clients learn to better self-regulate, we can then use our other traditional techniques to help clients challenge and process thoughts and feelings more efficiently. In other terms, we need to stretch before doing any type of exercise, and with the brain it is no different. We need to "stretch" the brain, or help regulate it and get it working efficiently, before there is going to be those great results from the traditional talk therapy.

We have offered in this applied science book many opportunities to integrate neurocounseling interventions into your counseling work. Our final paragraphs will discuss how you might want to create your own personalized Mind Room to house some of the interventions we have previously shared. The readers might want their own Mind Room or even be willing to assist clients to create their brain space or Mind Room.

Adapted from an article for LinkedIn, Pacheco (2020) discusses Mind Rooms as a popular method for athletes to stay at the top of their games. A Mind Room is a designated space for athletes to strengthen their mind-body connection and improve performance. They are equipped with cutting-edge technology relaxation and biofeedback devices. However, Mind Rooms don't have to be only for athletes. Anyone could become an Everyday Olympian, whether that be the top performers or leaders. Everyone could benefit from creating their own Mind Room.

Depending on the level of sophistication of the equipment (and staff to run and monitor the equipment), Mind Rooms can become quite expensive, but you do not need to spend a fortune to create your own Mind Room. We offer you suggestions to set up your own Mind Room, along with the names of relaxation apps and devices that fall on the less expensive end.

The Space

Find a quiet and calming location for your Mind Room. Having a space where you can have a few minutes of uninterrupted privacy is crucial. Ideally, this is your current office space. Next, place a comfortable chair or sofa in this room. I find recliner chairs with a head support work best. The important factor is that you can stretch out with your body and feel supported. The room does not need to be completely dark, but the ability to dim the lights and create a comfortable, relaxing tone is helpful. If it is a brighter room, you may find using an eye pillow useful to help block out some of the light.

The Equipment

The equipment for your Mind Room should fit with your relaxation goals, budget, and the amount of time you have available. Relaxation benefits can be experienced in five minutes or less. However, some programs that you want may take 20, 30, or more minutes to complete. Listed below are apps, programs, and equipment that we have found to be useful in our work (and we do not have any financial disclosures or connections to them). They are listed in order of price.

- Breathe2Relax ($0): This is a free app to use on your iPhone, iPad, and Apple Watch. It focuses on diaphragmatic breathing for relaxation. You can adjust the length of your inhale and exhale. The screen shows the breath pacer, visual images, and there is a voice to guide you through the breathing. The auditory guide allows you to close your eyes and still follow the breathing pace. For most individuals, the goal is to breathe approximately 6 breaths per minute (a 10-second inhale/exhale cycle). The 10-second cycle breaks down into a 4-second inhale and a 6-second exhale. The important factor is to have a longer exhale than inhale. This breathing pattern increases the "rest and digest" system (also called the parasympathetic nervous system) and decreases the stress response system (sympathetic nervous system).
- Belly Bio ($0): With this breathing app, you actually put the device on your abdomen and it tracks your breathing rate.
- Breath Pacer ($1): Similar to the Breathe2Relax app, but for a small fee.

- Digital Stress Thermometer ($25): The temperature of your hands can be an excellent indicator of your relaxation level. As you become relaxed, cool and tense hands become warm. After several minutes of relaxation, finger temperatures as low as in the 70s (Fahrenheit) can increase to the 90s.
- emWave2 ($200) and the Inner Breath trainer ($130–150): The emWave is a portable device that tracks your heart rate. Based on your heart rate, a breathing pacer is produced for you to follow. The red light indicates that you are not following the pacer or not in the ideal heart rate variability zone. The blue light indicates that you are following the pacer, but can do better. The green light means that you are following the pacer perfectly and increasing your heart rate variability to improve emotional and mental function. The Inner Breath Pacer is less expensive than the emWave and used with a free app downloaded to your smart device.
- The Muse2 ($220): The Muse devices help track the amount of time the brain is calm and help guide your meditation practice. You receive points for increasing the amount of time your mind is calm and relaxed. A soft headband to wear with the Muse is now available.

There are many devices available for purchase and this list is not exhaustive. Many of these are available in your app or Google store, Amazon, or directly from the company (e.g., HeartMath for the emWave devices).

We will end this chapter and text coming full circle, back to the beginning. We hope you are more equipped with knowledge, applied techniques, and a plan of action to begin or continue integrating neurocounseling into your counseling world.

Conclusions

This final chapter reiterates the many benefits of integrating neurocounseling and neuroscience into your clinical work. Neurocounseling adds value to your already existing profession by widening the array of interventions and knowledge base. It also widens your treatment team and offers even greater opportunities for success for your clients. The brain is the final frontier, and every day research offers us new and additional information about the brain and bodily connections. Join us in this ever-expanding neurocounseling journey. May the information and techniques in this practical text help you feel even more successful and intentional with your clients!

References

Broadwell, R. (ed.) (1995). *Neuroscience, Memory and Language*. New York: Basic Books.

Chapin, T. & Russell-Chapin, L. (2014). *Neurotherapy and Neurofeedback: Brain-based treatment for psychological and behavioral problems*. New York: Routledge.

Field, T.A., Jones, L.K. & Russell-Chapin, L. (2017). *Neurocounseling: Brain-based clinical approaches*. Alexandria, VA: American Counseling Association.

Hebb, D.O. (1949). *The Organization of Behavior: A neuropsychological theory*. New York: John Wiley and Sons.

Pacheco, N. (2020, February). *The Mind Room*. Linkedin.

Russell-Chapin, L. (2016). Integrating neurocounseling into the counseling profession: An introduction. *Journal of Mental Health Counseling* 38, 93–102. http://dx.doi.org/1017744/mehc.38.2.01.

Russell-Chapin, L. & Chapin, T. (2020). Neuroscience and the brain: What mental health counselors need to know. In Joshua C. Watson & Michael K. Schmit, *Introduction to Clinical Mental Health Counseling: Contemporary issues*. Los Angeles: SAGE.

Strack, B., Linden, M. & Wilson, V. (2011). *Biofeedback and Neurofeedback Applications in Sport Psychology*. Wheat Ridge, CO: Association for Applied Psychophysiology and Biofeedback.

INDEX